LIFE STORY WORK

Why, what, how and when

Tony Ryan and Rodger Walker

coramBAAF
ADOPTION & FOSTERING ACADEMY

Published by
CoramBAAF Adoption and Fostering Academy
41 Brunswick Square
London WC1N 1AZ
www.corambaaf.org.uk

Coram Academy Limited, registered as a company limited by guarantee
in England and Wales number 9697712, part of the Coram group, charity
number 312278

British Library Cataloguing in Publication Data

A catalogue record for this book is available from the British Library

ISBN 978 1 910039 41 0

Project management by Shaila Shah, Director of Publications, CoramBAAF
Designed and typeset by Helen Joubert Design
Printed in Great Britain by The Lavenham Press

Trade distribution by Turnaround Publisher Services, Unit 3, Olympia
Trading Estate, Coburg Road, London N22 6TZ

Contents

Notes about the authors

Tony Ryan formally retired in 2005 but continued to work in adoption assessment and training. Prior to retirement, he was Adoption Team Manager for Catholic Care, Diocese of Leeds and had been Principal Fostering and Adoption Officer in the Department of Social Service, Leeds City Council. With his late wife Margaret, they fostered eleven children over the years and is still in contact with some of them, the eldest now in his fifties.

Rodger Walker formerly managed the fostering and adoption services for Leeds City Council. Previously, he was Principal Training Officer for the department. He is now semi-retired and provides training and support in life story work for Orchard Care, an independent fostering agency.

Other contributors

Authors who contributed chapters to the previous edition, and which are reproduced in this one, include Ann Atwell, Maureen Hitcham, Jean Lovie and Gerrilyn Smith. Authors who have contributed new material for this edition published in 2016 include Gillian Shotton, Simon P Hammond, Sarah Ryan, Alison Horrox and Emma Hall.

Acknowledgements

We are not the first people to use life story work in work with children, and we thank all those whose ideas we have used in developing our practice.

The origins of our interest in life story work lie in our practice in the 1980s when we worked in a team which recruited people to adopt older and complex children. We were looking for a way to prepare older children for adoption and came across Claudia Jewett's book, *Adopting Older Children*, in which she described the use of life story books in relation to preparing a child to move on.

Since then we – and others – have developed the idea and used life story work successfully and developed its use in other areas of social work. Some of these developments are described in this book by the people who have carried out the work and we much admire their dedication and insight in adapting life story work. We recognise all the work done by others in this area of social work. We would also like to acknowledge all the children who helped us practise life story work and who were helped by the experience.

We would like to thank those people in other countries who have championed our work, and which has led to the previous edition of *Life Story Work* being translated and published in several countries. Finally, our thanks to CoramBAAF for the support and encouragement we have received.

Tony Ryan and Rodger Walker, February 2016

This edition

We are pleased to publish this new and comprehensively revised and updated edition of *Life Story Work*. This bestselling guide has been in print since 1992 and was preceded by *Making Life Story Books*, by the same authors and first published by BAAF in 1985. *Life Story Work* has now become an integral part of work with looked after children, helping them come to terms with past experiences, providing continuity of their life histories, and preparing them to move on to foster or adoptive families. As the practice has developed in recent decades, it has embraced the use of electronic multi-media options, but previously tried and tested techniques remain.

BAAF has also published other resources which can be used in a practical way with children. These include *My Life and Me*, by Jean Camis – a life story book for children and young people to fill in – and *Life Story Work: What it is and what it means*, by Shaila Shah and Hedi Argent – a guide for children explaining and describing life story work and its uses and benefits.

More recently, we published *Digital Life Story Work* by Simon Hammond and Neil Cooper, an innovative guide on using technology to help young people make sense of their experiences. BAAF also distributes *My Life Story*, by Bridget Betts and Afshan Ahmad, produced by Information Plus – an interactive computer-aided programme for children and young people to use. These resources are described in greater detail at the end of this book.

Shaila Shah, 2016

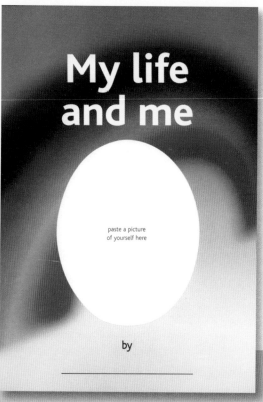
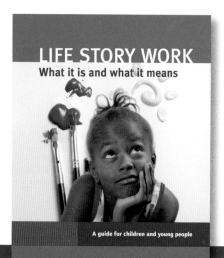

Introduction

Since we started writing about life story work in the 1980s and developing its use, inspired by Vera Fahlberg and Claudia Jewett, it has become a firmly established part of social work practice with looked after children. It is also now a requirement of recent legislation on adoption in England and Wales. Social workers in other countries have also become interested in the concept and practice, and previous editions of *Life Story Work* have been published in German, Serbo-Croat, Hungarian, Czech and Japanese.

Children themselves have asked for the information that the life story work process seeks to elicit and establish. In a booklet written by the Children's Rights Director in England, following a survey in 2006 of what children want from adoption, amongst the top seven things children listed was to be told about their past, including:

1 why they couldn't stay with their birth family and so were adopted;

2 details about their birth family;

3 other information the individual child asked about;

4 information about their own life before they were adopted;

5 where they were born;

6 if they had any brothers or sisters living somewhere else, and why they were split up;

7 whether they could make contact with their birth family.

(Commission for Social Care Inspection, 2006)

All these questions can and should be answered as part of the life story work process, as they help the child establish a sense of self and personal history.

As the potential for multimedia to be used has developed, it has become necessary to talk about the life story work process rather than life story books, because all sorts of formats can now be used, including audio, visual and digital. However, it is possible to do this work without actually producing a finished product of any kind since it is the process, rather than just the outcome, that is important. A record, however, is useful not only for the child and others to refer back to but also as an information record of the child's life.

Since the first publication of *Making Life Story Books* in 1985, there have been major developments in social work, that have resulted in changes in practice and emphasis, particularly in working with children and young people. Changes in legislation have only served to accentuate that listening to children and respecting their views and wishes is central to these developments, as it is central to life story work. The Adoption and Children Act 2002 (England and Wales) highlights the importance of the views of children and requires that, on placement for adoption, they must be given comprehensive information about themselves, underlining the

1

fact that some form of life story work needs to have been carried out with children before they are placed for adoption. Elsewhere in the UK, although there may not be the legislative basis for this, good practice requires that life story work be carried out. Recent research suggests that often this work is not carried out adequately, leaving a lot of ground to be covered when the child starts asking about their birth family and questioning their own identity. Whilst adoption usually ensures that some form of life story work is carried out, this is not usually the case for children achieving permanency through long-term fostering.

Although life story work is no longer regarded as a new concept, we have seen its progression in becoming central to planning and preparing for successful adoption and fostering placements. Whilst it is integral to good quality social work, it can also contribute to reducing disruptions and fits in with the Government's objectives of securing children in stable families as the best outcome for children in state care. Interestingly, internationally life story work is of particular interest in countries where child care policy is moving away from placing children in institutional care to permanent family-based care.

Even though carrying out life story work is not a requirement in legislation in Scotland or Northern Ireland, the need to take account of children's wishes and feelings *is* required by legislation, and good practice demands that this be central to social work with children separated from their birth families and requiring substitute families. In recent years, as the need for continued contact with birth family members, where appropriate, has also been recognised and integrated into practice, it is clear that children need to be equipped to deal with the challenges of this continuing contact. The growth of kinship care (also called friends and family care, or connected persons care) presents another area where the issue of identity needs to be addressed. Life story work is ideal for this, giving the child an opportunity to get accurate information about their birth family and examine their feelings about them, understand their troubled past and why they had to be separated from their family of origin, and have the chance of building a secure future. The increase in the adoption of older children also places particular demands upon adopters in requiring them to acknowledge a child's past and everything that it brings to the present. Adoption is a life-long process, not something that has an impact at only one moment in time.

Life story work has its place in all these developments and this revised edition reflects this. Life story work may not, however, always be the most appropriate way to help a child, and decisions as to when and how it can help should obviously be based on practice wisdom and experience and ideally made after consultation with colleagues.

Life story work is a way of working, it is not a therapeutic model. We are concerned to hear of inappropriate applications, where, for example, a child's circumstances demand skilled and long-term therapy, but life story work is used instead, perhaps because resources do not permit the child's needs to be properly met.

Please don't take on life story work, or any work with children, until you understand how to do it and you have the space and time to do it – we owe it to children to take as much care as possible.

Developments in information technology and social networking present both a rich source of information, images and contacts but also a potential danger from figures from the past with whom contact could be harmful and destabilising. There has been evidence (Fursland, 2010, 2013) that children have used social networking to contact their birth families and suffered emotional damage because they had not been prepared for this contact in a way that gave a realistic picture of why they were no longer with their birth families and had developed their own back story, which pictured their birth families as victims and as misunderstood. Life story work needs to equip children with a real picture of what happened when they left their birth families and help children to understand that not all parents can be adequate at parenting and that sometimes they can even be a threat to their children.

We can take some steps to protect children from some of the dangers of social networking but we cannot hope to keep them from finding ways to go online. The best protection is to be open and honest with them about the positives and negatives and develop a dialogue that enables them to tell you about their online activity and get your support and protection.

We hope that practitioners and those interested in using life story work to help children will continue to find this guide useful in helping children come to terms with their past experiences, understand changes in their lives, and adjust to a new life in a new family.

This book has been revised and updated to take into account developments and changes in practice, legislation and terminology.

1 Why do life story work?

Children who live with their birth families have the opportunity to know about their past, and have a means of being able to understand it through discussions with their parents and others and to clarify past events in terms of the present. Children separated from their birth families are often denied this opportunity; they may have moved between placements, social workers, homes and neighbourhoods. Their past may be lost, much of it even forgotten.

When children lose track of their past, they may well find it difficult to develop emotionally and socially. If adults cannot or do not discuss this past with them, it is reasonable for children to suppose that it may be bad.

Remember also that children have a right to see their files. Finding out what happened to them, particularly abuse, can be a potentially destabilising shock, if they have not had the opportunity beforehand to learn about this, discuss and clarify what happened, and share their feelings about it

What is life story work?

Life story work is an attempt to give back some of this past to children separated from their family of origin. Gathering together facts about that life and the significant people in it helps them begin to accept their past and go forward into the future with this knowledge. We have found that most children separated in this way gain a great deal from talking about their past, present and future to a sympathetic adult. Life story work provides a structure for talking to children. In fact, both children and adults looking after or working with them can gain benefits from such a process. Interesting work has been carried out by social workers with adults (an example is mentioned in the booklist) who need to experience attention-giving and be given help in orientating themselves. Similarly, elderly people gain a great deal from "reminiscence therapy", and Age Concern, now Age UK, has produced a very helpful pack for work with groups of people, illustrating the power of nostalgia and affirming people's sense of identity.

Children separated from their birth parents, whether they are in a residential unit, with foster carers, or going to a permanent new family or returning to their birth family, need to understand why the separation occurred and why various adults have been unable to care for them. Sometimes children return to their birth family after a long separation and some useful work has been done with both the returning child and the birth family to clarify the past and increase the chances for a successful return. Our experience with the children with whom we have worked has encouraged us to believe that life story work is a useful way of fulfilling these needs, and that all the children have benefited in some way.

Life story work may result in a book or DVD, a computer file or memory stick, or simply be a record of sessions that took place. It does not have to result in a product – it is the process rather than just the product that will yield most benefits for the children and young people involved; the product will be the "record".

All children are entitled to an accurate knowledge of their past and their family. This is a right that children who are secure in their families take for granted. For those children separated from their birth families, the right to this knowledge is equally important, not only for the sake of the children themselves, but also for their own children.

Life story work can usefully be adapted, not only to suit elderly people, but also the parents from whom children are separated. Many parents whose children are currently being looked after have been in the care system themselves. The possibility of someone having done life story work with them is remote. However, if it is carried out with them as adults, it may help clarify the reasons, for both children and parents, for the family not being able to live together, and in so doing make best use of the separation.

The Adoption and Children Act 2002 (England and Wales) laid stress on the need for children to be involved in discussions that affect their lives. Life story work can be a means of giving the child age-appropriate information that allows them to make these informed decisions. For example, the child who discloses the identity of an adult in the birth family home who has sexually abused him or her will need to understand that it may not be possible to return home while this situation prevails.

Life story work should complement the underlying philosophy of the Adoption and Children Act 2002 – of participation and involvement of the child and his or her family.

What do children get from life story work?

Life story work gives children a structured and understandable way of talking about themselves. It can produce clarity where there are dangerous or idealised fantasies. Once completed, it provides them with a record which they and, with their agreement, the adults caring for them can refer to at any time, particularly when there is a crisis.

Life story work can increase a child's sense of self-worth and self-esteem because, sadly, at the back of the minds of nearly all children separated from their families of origin is the thought that they are worthless and unlovable. They blame themselves for the actions of adults. If they have been abandoned, neglected or injured by their parents or other family members, they are convinced that they brought it upon themselves.

Another aspect of this feeling is described by Kate Cairns (2002) who reports that some children feel so intrinsically "bad" that they feel that talking about themselves may "contaminate" other people. You, the worker, need to make it clear to the child that you are the adult and can cope with the child's expressions of emotion connected with trauma and pain.

Life story work provides an opportunity to show children why they should be proud of themselves, and this positive attitude should be evident in any book, film or other record that results. In talking about their birth parents, for example, although you may tell them a suitably-worded version of the truth (however painful that may be) about their family and why they are being looked after, it is important to stress the positive side. You need to talk about their birth parents in non-judgemental terms. Perhaps you might say that not everybody is good at being a parent, but that does not mean they are bad in other respects.

When you have worked together on a child's life story, you will feel much closer to the child. We have found that memories of our own childhoods are always awoken. If we, too, have experienced pain, we share this with the child – while always remembering whose story it is! Some people do life story work with more than one child at a time, and some sharing of experiences – without breaking confidences, of course – can make a child feel better. Thus a child can appreciate that many people experience pain in their childhood and that the fault does not lie with them; they need not feel guilt or responsible, as so many children amazingly do, for their parents' behaviour.

Finally, you and the child need to be able to relax and enjoy at least some parts of each of the sessions and, for this, you may need to re-learn how to play. This is a chance to have a lot of fun! With some of the play techniques suggested later on, you will need to get down on the floor with the child and play with toys. Self-consciousness is not a virtue in this situation but, if you need a reason, you should know that your playing has a serious purpose and is a valuable technique, and is as important as being able to talk naturally to a child about important issues. While not all life story work will lead you into play, some will, and you might as well enjoy yourself while playing!

About identity

A healthy sense of one's identity is vital to everybody. A poor sense of identity can block the development of children and adults alike, and limit their ability to take on fresh challenges. For some children, one of the major challenges of their life will be moving into a new family. At its worst, a poor sense of identity can "freeze" children so they have an over-investment in the past and cannot move on to think about the future. It can also cause apathy and a depressed, fatalistic outlook.

Identity is a complex concept; it probably starts in individuals with the first separation of the "inside" and "outside" selves at about six months. This creation of the idea of "self" is crucial to healthy development and where it is hindered by events and by other people who are important (like mothers and fathers) not responding appropriately, severe problems can arise.

Whilst an understanding of the "self" is difficult, particularly for children severed from their roots and without a clear future, it is made easier by separating out some of the more easily definable parts and discussing them openly with a child. One way of doing this is to talk about the past, the present and the future.

The past is made up of places, significant dates and times, people, changes, losses or separations and other events, both happy and sad, like illnesses, holidays and birthdays.

The present is made up of self-images, reactions to the past and responses to questions like: What am I doing here? Where do I belong? How do others see me?

The future is made up of issues such as: What will I be? Where will I live? What chances do I have? What other changes will there be?

Many children we have worked with have felt miserable and depressed. Looking to the future should be about easing these feelings and replacing them with hopes and aspirations. In life story work with a child, issues relating to the past, present and future can be raised in ways that feel natural to a child. This will give you and the child opportunities to establish facts about the past and present and go some way towards demystifying events and people in the child's life. Similarly, hopes and doubts about the future can be raised and "bridging" (linking the past to the future) into the new family or situation can begin.

This section on identity theory is necessarily brief and you may want to read more authoritative views – we have listed books for further reading at the end of this book.

The psychology of life story work

We do not regard life story work as a standalone psychotherapeutic technique (although it has its place as part of some techniques). However, it does offer some insights into understanding the effect on children's identities of being separated from their early carers.

Gillian Shotton is a specialist educational psychologist who sometimes uses life story work as part of her practice and has written papers on the effects of life story work in later life on both adopters and adopted people.

We include below an excerpt from her dissertation (University of Newcastle, 2012), which looks at life story work from a psychologist's point of view. It also looks briefly at why some writers on children see life story work as effective in helping children to be more in control of their past.

Gillian Shotton is an Educational Psychologist working as part of the multi-disciplinary North Northumberland Locality Inclusion Support Team based in Alnwick, Northumberland.

Perspectives on the underlying psychology of life story work

There is a number of theories and perspectives on the psychology that underlies life story work. Aust (1981) writes about life story work as being the beginning of a re-education of the child's beliefs in a manner congruent with Ellis' Rational Emotive Therapy (1977). She describes how a child's reaction to separation and loss produces painful feelings of anger, abandonment, shame and rejection. These feelings affect how children see themselves and distort their interpretation of events. They commonly come to believe themselves to be bad and unlovable. Life story work is thought to help in identifying, challenging and re-educating these beliefs.

The trauma of rejection and separation impacting on the child's sense of worth is also outlined by Harper (1996). She puts forward the view that life story work can help children to accept their past and as a consequence they can then feel in control of it, rather than it controlling them. In this way they can move on, putting the past behind them. This links in with ideas around developing a sense of agency or self-efficacy (Bandura, 1977). Harper uses a non-directive play therapy approach to life story work, rooted in psychotherapy.

The work of Bowlby (1980, 1988) on separation and attachment is acknowledged by Henry (2005) as providing a foundation for understanding how children experience and respond to loss. The model she outlines focuses on issues of loss, identity, attachment, and safety. The underlying thinking is that the child needs to reconcile the traumas and separations in their life in order to make a successful transition to a permanent placement. The child must also be allowed to grieve the losses they have experienced (Bowlby, 1980, 1988), and much of the difficult, acting-out and aggressive behaviour, often seen in looked after children, is understood as being due to unresolved loss. Life story work is seen as being a useful tool for helping children to reconcile the traumas they have experienced and grieve their losses which will then help them to be able to move on.

The model of life story work put forward by Cooke-Cotton and Beck (2007) is rooted in narrative psychology. They draw on theory put forward by Nelson and Fivush (2004) outlining how the family and cultural stories that children hear, help them construct their own autobiographical narrative and thus contribute to their sense of identity, helping them to make sense of their past, present and anticipated future (Nelson and Fivush, 2004; McLean, 2005). Parents reminiscing, telling their children stories about times in their earlier lives, provide children with information about who they are and this then helps to develop their sense of self.

For younger children, autobiographical remembering relies on the parent/carer prompting and sustaining the focus of the conversation (Habermas and Bluck, 2000). The years between complete dependence on the carer and the individual being able to independently construct their own memories are described by Nelson and Fivush (2004) as the years of co-constructed memories. Parents help the child to construct a coherent life narrative, so that they develop a clear understanding about where they came from, how others felt about them, their place in the family and in the world. There is evidence to suggest that reminiscences and the co-construction of life memories may be related to secure attachment, the development of a sense of self in the past, and how past self relates to current self (Fivush and Vasudeva, 2002; Fivush, Reese and Haden, 2006; Kulkofsky and Koh, 2009). A critical review of research into carer–child reminiscence is outlined in the next section. The life story is sculpted continuously, becoming the organising structure that carries the self (Cook-Cottone and Beck, 2007).

Children in care do not live with people who can verify their past and so miss out on the opportunity to create a positive and coherent life narrative (Beste and Richardson, 1981). Life story work is seen as helping to fill the gap; the work allows for reminiscing and the co-construction of a coherent life narrative which will then help the child develop a stronger sense of identity.

Narrative and psychodynamic ideas are drawn upon by Treacher and Katz (2001). A central proposal is that identity is multifaceted, inherently conflicting and constantly developing. They put forward the view that narratives and fantasies in adoption (and in life generally) help individuals express their feelings, thoughts and confusions. Alongside this they also recognise that narratives and myths can trap individuals into not allowing different thoughts, feelings and perceptions to occur. Life story books are thought to sometimes silence the difficulties experienced by adoptees by not allowing them enough space for exploring troublesome feelings and fantasies. They outline how often the life story that is constructed adheres to a prevailing narrative that has the following basic elements:

- Your birth parents loved you but because of their personal circumstances they were not able to look after you

- Your adoptive parents chose you because they love and value you

- You have had terrible life experiences and our job is to help you overcome those experiences

The writers outline how often such narratives prevail in order to help the professional make sense of the pain the child has been through. They point out that the story is unlikely to mention how administrative mistakes, a lack of available carers or practice failures have led to difficulties for the child. A certain type of narrative is expected to emerge which is essentially positive and reparative but which may not be the most helpful, or tell certain aspects of the story.

It is useful and interesting to look at the differing perspectives regarding the psychology underlying life story work. My own interpretation is that none of the perspectives seem to be in conflict but rather each offers a slightly different emphasis or way of understanding how life story work might function. In line with Ellis' rational emotional therapy, life story work has the potential to impact on children's beliefs about themselves. From a psychotherapy perspective, life story work also has the capacity to help children accept and understand their past and feel more in control of it, developing their sense of agency and so allowing them to move on.

This is what happened to me, this is my story. I am responsible for some parts of my story and others are responsible for other parts.

Papers by Gillian Shotton have appeared in *Adoption & Fostering* and may be useful in understanding how life story work can help adopted children and young people if carried out properly.

Drawing on Bowlby's work, life story work has the facility to help the child reconcile the traumas and separations they have experienced and allow them to grieve their losses. From a narrative perspective, life story work has the potential to help looked after children develop a coherent life narrative so contributing to their sense of self. It is likely that each child's experience of life story work will be quite different and may work in all, some, one or perhaps none of these ways depending on how the work is carried out, by whom, in what context and at what stage of a child's life.

Extracted from *"Remember when..." Exploring the experiences of looked after children and their carers in engaging in collaborative reminiscence*, by Gillian Shotton (published as a thesis by University of Newcastle, 2012, available at: https://theses.ncl.ac.uk/dspace/bitstream/10443/1685/1/Shotton%2012.pdf)

Who should do life story work with children?

We firmly believe in the healing effect of talking. Any sympathetic adult who is prepared to spend the time and give the commitment to the child by doing life story work and making a life story book, DVD, memory card, stick or any lasting record to which the child can add and refer back to, can be the right person to do it. We have experience of foster carers and adopters being very successful in doing life story work and some of that work is described in the chapter on rehabilitation.

Anyone who takes on this task will need to enlist the active support of the child's social worker and significant others through regular discussions. We have successfully helped adoptive parents and foster carers and many residential social workers to work with children in this way. It is also important – as the spirit of the Adoption and Children Act 2002 encourages – to make a genuine attempt to include the birth family, although the child will always be the guide as to the extent of their involvement.

Any social worker wanting to undertake this work will need the permission to spend the necessary time with the child and get their supervisor's support. They will need to understand the complexity of the task and be clear about their role and their commitment to working with the child.

What does life story work require of you?

Children in foster care and adoption are on a journey, and many parts of it are difficult. They need to feel that someone is with them on that journey, and they need a framework to help them think about it and feel safe.

(Schofield and Beek, 2006)

To embark on this journey with the child, above all you need time, sensitivity, empathy for the child and a commitment to the work. An ability to listen to the child and understand them is paramount; the skills and particular techniques can be learnt (as this guide shows you in later chapters) and experience will come with practice. There is a useful guide for children, *Life Story Work: What it is and what it means* (Shah and Argent, 2006), which could be read with the child to explain the process and why it is important.

Whoever undertakes life story work with the child needs to be alert and have patience in order to pick up any clues that the child may reveal, particularly during sessions when not a lot is happening because the child is not in the mood or is testing you to see if you can be trusted. The person also needs to be sensitive to the child. There is no blueprint for life story work, but the child is always the key. It is your responsibility to find ways of letting the child tell you about his or her life, and avoid imposing your own views. Whilst you should not allow patently false information to be recorded, you also need to avoid taking over and producing the "authorised version" of a child's life. It is the child's life story after all, and it is how he or she views it that is important.

It is also important to convey to the child that the record can be altered. Some children will disclose important information at a later date, which they will wish to add to their life story.

There are mistakes that less experienced workers sometimes make but which can, with common sense, easily be avoided.

1   Never betray the child's confidences made to you except in exceptional circumstances as mentioned below.

2   Do not avoid talking about things the child wants to talk about because they make you uncomfortable.

3 Do not put words into the child's mouth.

4 Once you have taken on life story work, you must not abandon the child halfway through it and hope that someone else can complete your work. You should continue with it until both of you agree it is time to end your regular sessions.

5 Never use either the end product or carrying out life story work as a prize or a punishment, but only as a normal part of your life or relationship together.

6 Go at the child's pace, not yours – it's actually quicker this way! Rushing children only makes them slow down or skimp on details. In this busy world it may be necessary to have time-limited sessions that provide a framework that the child can cope with and more easily manage.

7 Be consistent and reliable – the child has to know when you are coming. If you can't make it, let the child know as far in advance as possible, preferably personally by phone or Skype. Don't start work and then say you'll be back when you've got time. A child will not trust you and will feel hurt if you do this. Remember, if you can't make a session, tell the child as soon as possible.

To be effective, you will need to engage yourself with the process and thus be able to show empathy and engagement. This can take a lot out of the worker and may evoke painful memories for them – it is crucial that you have supervision to give you the chance to talk these issues through.

It should be made clear at the start of life story work that if the child discloses abuse of themselves and other children or anything that puts them in danger, some information will have to be passed on to those adults responsible for their protection (see also Chapter 13, *Working with children who have been sexually abused*).

When might you do life story work?

Before a start is made you might like to ask yourself the following questions.

Are you the right person to do this work?	Yes/No
Is your agency committed to this work?	Yes/No
Can you get the training and support needed?	Yes/No
Are the roles of everyone contributing clear?	Yes/No
Do you have life story work planning meetings?	Yes/No
Who will be working with the child?	
Actions to be taken:	

Life story work can be started at any time when the adult and the child have enough confidence in each other to begin and the time to continue. Sometimes it is part of preparing a child who is going from a residential unit to a family; sometimes it can help the child accept life as it is. It can of course be used to prepare a child to return home and can be used both with the child and the family. We include a chapter in this book that describes an excellent piece of work where a child was returned to his mother successfully using life story work methods – see Chapter 15.

Ideally, the decision to do life story work will come at a review or case conference – in fact, the role of the Independent Reviewing Officer is to oversee that the necessary information is collected as a prerequisite to life story work being done. At the same time, it will be decided who does what and where.

Before beginning, you will need to have a planning meeting with others involved with the child, for example, the carer/parent, the child's teacher, the social worker (if you are not the social worker), etc. This is important in order to prepare others for reactions from the child, such as regression, and to get as many sources of information as possible.

Sometimes this work is directed by the court and time limits are specified by the courts. Occasionally, life story work is done to meet court requirements without engaging the child. This is not life story work, but simply a biography of the child to meet a legal requirement. If this occurs, it may be necessary to engage the Children's Guardian or otherwise speak to the court to point out the limitations of such a process.

Everyone involved should then support undertaking the work, feeding you with facts and information and suggesting ways around problems. Life or child appreciation days (Sayers and Roach, 2011) can help by filling in a lot of gaps, which will help with the life story work (see later in this chapter for more information about these). A foster carer or adoptive parent should look for support from their social worker and perhaps from other substitute parents, and have regular discussions about progress. Equally, if you are a social worker or residential social worker, good supervision is very important.

It is important to have a framework that the child can use and understand that lays out the length and frequency of the session, the venue, etc. This framework can be negotiated with the child before the work starts and can take the form of a simple "contract".

Other members of the "team" involved with the child who hear of the child progressing or regressing should discuss this with the adult undertaking the life story work. They should also be prepared to cope with the child reliving past experiences or looking for reassurance and possibly displaying disturbed behaviour. They need to understand that this is all part of the healing process.

Feedback to the "team" is also useful in reaching appropriate decisions about the child's future. However, it is important to repeat the warning about not betraying the child's confidences to you.

How do you deal with confidentiality?

The question of keeping confidential what a child tells you while undertaking life story work together is an important one, and to which we have given much thought. Throughout the time we have worked with children we have tried to reach a satisfactory solution to the conflict between not betraying the child's trust and yet needing to share some of the information with others.

One of the difficulties is that the significant adults in the child's life, such as foster carers, social workers and residential social workers, may have a "team" approach. They will feel that it is important to pool knowledge with the goal of helping the child. The child, of course, may not regard this in the same way. We have always found in our individual work with children that they want the discussions to remain confidential to us. Children may disclose something of their inner world that they are not prepared even to record in a life story book. For example, they may express anger against a person in their past that may have relevance for the future and you may feel it necessary to pass it on to others. In such circumstances, we would share the outline of the confidence only, without disclosing any details.

We always make it clear to the significant adults that their child will probably demand confidentiality about certain things and that we intend to respect this. It may be possible to explain to the child that you would like permission to talk to others about a particular disclosure because you believe it may help him or her. You might be able to negotiate with the child what you are allowed to say. This in itself can be helpful to the child because it provides another format to discuss a possible painful event in the past. However, disclosures are sometimes so serious that you cannot keep silent, for instance, if the child knows of a sexual abuser still actively abusing children. You can think of other instances yourself relating to issues of safeguarding, protection and self-harm.

In such cases, you will have to explain to the child that you must share information in order to protect him or her and/or other children. What you can promise is that you will not share the information unless absolutely necessary, that you will stand by the child, be present at any interviews, and assure the child that he or she will be protected from any abuse. You can also, within reason, agree with the child the timing of sharing the disclosure. In general, the only thing that stops a child disclosing abuse is a belief that nobody can help or protect them. A child will disclose to you if you gain his or her trust – be careful not to betray that trust.

How does life story work end?

There comes a stage when you both agree that you have reached the present day and covered everything you can, and that the regular sessions can end. This point is different for every child. However, you should be suspicious if the life story work has turned into little more than a photograph album and you are finished after only three or four sessions. In that situation, go back over what has been produced, and see if the child can write or draw about any particular period which you know (from the file or from having completed a questionnaire, as described later) to be sensitive.

We never regard the work as finished as life goes on, but some record of the process is important as it provides a reference point, particularly as it can be updated until adulthood. It can be turned to in a crisis, such as when a child revives a ghost or a myth from the past, or is beginning to discover and remember parts of the childhood not available to them when they started on their life story work. Then you can go to the section of the book or video, etc, that dealt with it and gently rediscover or redefine the reality together.

We often find, for example, that when we discuss a new permanent family with a child, he or she will start to make up fantasies about their birth family, however badly they were let down by them. Children have a natural fear of letting go of their present relative security – however unsatisfactory that may be – to face a risky future. Life story work can be helpful in looking back together at the anger the child felt about the birth parents when originally doing the work; this may help him or her to let go more easily and face the future.

The welfare checklist

Courts now require social workers to have worked with a child to find out what the child might want to happen and why. In coming to a decision about the paramount interests of the child, a court will pay attention to the welfare checklist of the Children Act 1989, which is a list of the factors the court takes into account when considering the child's welfare throughout his/her life. There are similar requirements elsewhere in the UK.

Life story work can help a child and social worker to reach agreement on what to say to the court. We particularly point to the first four parts of the checklist mentioned below. The court must take into account:

1   the ascertainable wishes and feelings of the child concerned (considered in the light of his or her age and understanding);

2   his or her physical, emotional and educational needs;

3   the likely effect on him or her of any change in circumstances;

4   his or her age, sex, background and any characteristics that the court considers relevant.

Part 2 of the checklist requires the court to hear what the child's emotional needs are, and Part 3 highlights the need for a child to have thought through, with a social worker, what effect change will have on him or her. Agreeing what these are should be part and parcel of life story work. The Welfare Checklist for Adoption and Placement Proceedings of the Adoption and Children Act 2002 adds to the list the lifetime effect of having ceased to be a member of the original family and become an adopted person, and this must be considered along with the issue of any harm the child has suffered or is at risk of suffering, including impairment caused by seeing or hearing the ill-treatment of another. Life story work helps to focus on these aspects.

This book is the result of our own experience. We hope that what we have said here will help and not discourage you. You may worry that you might damage a child or give him or her too much pain. If you have a commitment to the child, you are the right person to undertake life story work and you will more than compensate in the long term for any pain the child might suffer in the short term. The only damage you can do is by walking away from your commitment before it is completed.

Painful issues for both child and worker inevitably will arise; nonetheless, research suggests that children need and want an understanding of the past and present and that this will help them move on with hope for the future.

2 Communicating with children

The following "Ten Commandments", quoted directly from *Opening New Doors* by Kay Donley, former Director of Spaulding for Children, an agency in the US, in our opinion "say it all" when it comes to communicating with children. While the terminology reflects the public care system in the USA, the message is universal.

1 **Avoid clichés when talking to children**

Children recognise clichés and your use of them will readily and clearly inform the child that you are indeed an adult who does not know how to talk to them. Some of the typical clichés that adults use in working with children are questions, probing questions, such as, 'How do you like school? Which class are you in?' Never begin a conversation with a child in that way. Eventually, when you really know the child, such questions may be appropriate, but never as an opening gambit. The best way to begin a conversation with a child is simply to exchange some pleasantries about who you are and how pleased you are to know him or her and let it go for a while. Children are more responsive to the idea of approaching you gradually, than to being physically and psychically overwhelmed by this large thing that flies at them and begins to probe their innermost thoughts. Take your time. You never know at first if you have a very shy, withdrawn child or a very aggressive one.

2 **Assume that any child you are going to work with has some deep concern that has never been adequately understood or answered**

I am referring specifically to children in public care, all of whom typically share the experience of having been separated from their parents. In many cases they have also lost a succession of carers – residential staff and foster carers. In working with the child you may, in fact, discover that someone very skilled and very sensitive has helped him to understand what has happened. But it is safer to assume that no one has adequately assessed the deep and often confused concerns of the child.

3 Understand from the beginning that children in care have been hurt; some part of them has been damaged

Never make the assumption that because everyone presents this child as untouched and undamaged, he or she must be that way. More often than not, the child will have been handled by a lot of unperceptive people. Perhaps this particular child has made an exceptionally good adjustment in the face of difficult and painful circumstances. But as a rule, there are always some damaged pieces of unfinished business tucked away. If you understand that, you will not be dismayed or thrown off balance six months later when someone says: 'You know, there's something peculiar about this kid. He's not quite what I would call "normal".'

4 Remember that, in working with a child, your essential task is to learn how he explains himself to himself, and what he understands his situation to be

Unless you really know what is going on inside him, you will not be able to represent him justly or truthfully to residential staff or to potential foster or adoptive parents. It is not simply that you must know where this child is for your own satisfaction. You must be prepared to communicate your understanding to other people. This is not easy.

5 Develop specific concrete tools that will help you communicate with children

Children are not normally interested solely in verbalisation as a way of communicating with anyone. They have other available tools and you must find out what they are so that you can use them too.

6 Be prepared to become a dependable, predictable and regular fixture in the child's experience

You simply cannot pop in on a Monday and say, 'I'll see you again sometime soon'. The social worker's indefinite promise of returning to his life usually means avoiding him for several weeks and then popping in again. This simply does not work and is, in fact, destructive. You are adding to the child's already increasing fund of knowledge that, as far as he is concerned, adults are undependable, unpredictable and unknowable. You must regularise your contact. Most social workers say, 'I really would like to, but I haven't the time'. This begs the question, because it is possible to regularise contacts, even if there are long intervals between visits. It is the idea of predictability that is important to the child. If you make a commitment then you keep it. (And I mean you keep it, even if it breaks your back!) If, for some reason, you are unable to keep the appointment you have made, it is important that you communicate directly with the child the reasons why you cannot. I have known workers go to the extent of sending a telegram to a child whom they could not reach by telephone, so strong was their sense of commitment.

7 **Remember that each child's experience is unique and that it is absolutely crucial that each child is helped to begin to come to grips with his life**

You cannot begin on the assumption that, because you have worked successfully with one or two children who have been neglected by their parents, you know what this experience means to any child. Certainly, you can learn from one situation and apply your knowledge to another. But keep in mind that you are dealing with individuals: deceptively similar experiences have very different meanings for different children.

8 **As you work with a child over a period of time, you must help him develop what I call a "cover story" ***

"Cover story" is not a very good phrase because a lot of people think that I mean concealing things and I do not. I believe that a child must have a clear, understandable, acceptable explanation of his circumstances, which he must be able to use at will and comfortably. For example, when he goes to a new school, he will be meeting a lot of new children, making friends and meeting people living in the neighbourhood. He will be asked questions about himself and it is essential that he should have a socially acceptable and logical explanation for who he is and where he is and why he is in this situation. Only too frequently, unskilled workers do not appreciate how essential this is and do not help the child develop a "cover story" for public consumption. Without it the child is left to his own devices and frequently falls into fabrication. A child fabricates when he is not quite sure how people will receive the true facts of his situation. Fabrication, once found out, will very quickly give the child a reputation in the neighbourhood for being a spinner of tall tales, or at worst, a liar.

* For children who have been sexually abused, it may be more helpful to think in terms of privacy of "good" and "bad" secrets. Such children may have a version of events in their life for public consumption, and one they share with significant and trusted adults.

9 **Commit yourself always to what I call a multifaceted or composite view of the child**

Remember there is no one true way of seeing and experiencing a youngster. Every person who has contact with the child will have a slightly different point of view and a unique experience. Some people will be enthusiastic about him, while others cannot abide him. What you are really searching for is a combination of all those perceptions, because buried amongst all of them there is the truth. Somewhere, amongst all those varying views of the child, will be a perception that his potential adoptive parents may make of him. So it is important that you begin to develop that kind of sensitivity and awareness.

10 **Keep in mind from the beginning of your work that you are obliged to convey to any carers – be they residential staff or adoptive families – a true sense of the child's history**

You may think that this is self-evident and that I am being needlessly repetitious in stressing this point. But I think it bears repeating, because many social workers feel they are doing a child a grave injustice by telling the full and sorry tale, and that the only way to spare the child is to conceal certain things. These are usually things the social worker finds distressing or unpalatable, so they are concealed because she feels that this will give the child a better chance in life, a better opportunity for placement, an easier adjustment. Invariably those very things come flashing up anew out of the child's history and past to create problems and difficulties for him and his caretakers. This is a painful area for most social workers but it is one which you must grapple with and come to terms with.

(Reproduced with kind permission from *Opening New Doors*, by Kay Donley)

Before you begin

The idea of life story work or life story activities should grow naturally if you talk and listen to what children say about their family and why they think they are separated from them. There are, however, guidelines that draw on Kay Donley's work as described in her "Ten Commandments" above.

1   The aim, both initially and throughout the duration of the life story work, is to show the child that you are interested in him or her and that there is no limit to what you can be told. You can make it clear that you would like to know lots more about him or her and so will be visiting regularly and getting to know them.

Remember that you are talking to a person who happens to be a child as well as a service user. This means that he or she is about as interested in telling you about how they are getting on at school as you would be in telling a stranger about how you are getting on at work. Every other adult will have asked them how they get on at school, and they know it is just a conversational ploy used by strangers. When you have got to know the child and he or she knows you are genuinely interested, they may tell you honestly how they feel about school.

You need not say anything of great meaning at first, but simply convey that you will be coming to talk to the child about him or herself and to perhaps make a book, or film, or tape recording about their life. Each child will work at a different pace, just like adults, and you should allow the work to happen naturally; any child will let you know when they want to be friends with you.

2   Should you feel the need to approach the idea of making a life story book or video cautiously or slowly, you could start with a questionnaire book, which we describe later.

3   When the life story work is undertaken by someone not living with the child, it should always take place at set times which you faithfully keep

to. Don't just say, 'I'll see you in a week or two'. Make a date and keep to it. If you cannot keep an appointment, ring up and speak to the child personally, say why you cannot come and say when you are going to come next. You will probably be the first person in the child's life to do this and it will bring forward the day when he or she learns to trust you.

4   If you are living with the child, you should be able to talk together at any time that is mutually convenient. In addition, there should be regular times set aside so that the child does not have to be responsible for continuing the work. You must not just allow the topic to drift and find that weeks go by without the work progressing.

5   **Life or Child Appreciation Day**

A Child Appreciation Day brings together those people who have had a significant role in a child's life so that they can together take a conducted and facilitated journey through the life of the child. It also helps to capture a chronological history of the major events, changes and moves in the child's life; understand the factors that have influenced the child's perceptions and reactions to events and circumstances; and capture stories and anecdotes about the child (Sayers and Roach, 2011).

We were first acquainted with the concept of a Life or Child Appreciation Day through the work of the adoption team at Gateshead Council.

Usually such a meeting takes place shortly after the adoptive parents have met the child, ideally during the introductory stage. Already in place will be the child's chronology and possibly their life graph. From these it should be possible to construct flowcharts prior to the meeting and, from this, to identify people who have been involved with the child. Obvious participants would be current carers, social worker, previous foster carers, nursery staff, school staff, and health visitor. There will be gaps in the information and often these gaps can be closed by a contribution that had not been forthcoming previously, for example, the child's key worker in the nursery, the cook at a family centre, a child minder, etc.

A Child Appreciation Day will provide an opportunity to understand how a child has made sense of his or her experiences. It can also help bring a child's individuality "to life" for their new substitute carers. Participants can be invited to bring photographs, toys and memorabilia. In this guided "journey", participants can recollect events and anecdotes which, in turn, can trigger a response from another, for example, where there may be concerns about a child's ability to attach. These could be allayed by foster carers describing the development of reciprocity between them and the child. Nonetheless, it is important that a pragmatic picture is given, which means negative information too, especially if this could unbalance the proposed placement.

At one meeting, where the child was four years old, and the youngest of five, the plan was for no direct contact with her siblings. This concerned her prospective adoptive parents who were prepared to participate in some form of face-to-face contact between the children. The social worker, who had been involved in the court proceedings, reported that a child psychologist, when questioned, had said that, in her opinion and experience, the family children were traumatised and the potential for harm through sexualised behaviour should they meet was too great a risk. From this came the suggestion of an annual "newsletter" that would include photographs of the children with their adoptive families, which would be collated by the agency's adoption support service.

By the close of the meeting, the adoptive parent's knowledge and understanding of the child's life was enhanced considerably and they felt better equipped to deal with the issues that faced them.

3 Before starting life story work

Initial research

You need to inform yourself about the child's "official" background before you start to work together. If you are a social worker, you will have access to the child's file. If you are an adoptive parent or foster carer, and it has been decided that you will be helping your child to do some life story work, then your child's social worker should provide the information to you. It is useful, wherever possible, to hold a Life or Child Appreciation Day (as discussed in Chapter 2). Remember to guard against just finding out about the child's mother and include the father's perspective too. Even absent fathers have an influence on what happened and they are equally responsible. Children want to know, where possible, about their birth father.

Don't be afraid to badger until you have all the information you need. If you encounter difficulties, exercise your right to call a review to "iron out" any problems.

Read the information about the child carefully and thoroughly. Collate the information in chronological order, noting the reasons given for decisions, the reasons for moves and so on. Make a note of any gaps in the records so that you can obtain information about these periods. From this research you will be able to construct a "life graph" for the child. We show an example in a later chapter, where we discuss life graphs in detail.

It may be at this stage that a worker discovers that there are indicators that might suggest a child has been sexually abused. Workers will then need to decide what to do with this information. It can be very helpful for looked after children who have not yet disclosed their experience of sexual abuse to have an adult "guess" that sexual abuse was something that was going on in their family of origin. Often no one has sat down and reviewed the whole of the child's file in this manner before. It is extremely important to ascertain whether or not a child has suffered harm, for example, if they have been sexually abused in their family of origin, before contacting the significant people in the child's life. Perpetrators will often go to great lengths to silence the children, and renewed contact can act as a trigger both for traumatic memories for the child, and for renewed attempts by the adults to silence the child again.

Using the information you have gathered, write immediately to significant people in the child's life. They may take time to respond and you want to have this information available when you need it. This task should be undertaken by the agency that has responsibility for the child. Explain about the life story work, and if a book is planned, ask for information and the loan of photographs and other documents. It is important to emphasise that photographs can be copied or scanned and returned to the sender, or that they can send copies, and digital photos can of course be emailed. We give below an example of the kind of letter that you might send in order to get such information. The material you ask for may well be very slow to arrive or may never arrive and you will have to depend upon other aids.

Mrs M Croft
7 New Town Estate
Westfield

Dear Mrs Croft

I have recently started visiting David to help him prepare a book about his life before he moved to live with (the foster or adoptive family). Already I have obtained several photographs for him to include but I have no photographs of when he was very young, nor any of you.

Photographs, I realise, are precious but nowadays they can easily be copied. If you have any photographs I would be grateful if you would loan them to me and I will return them as soon as I have obtained copies. If the photos you have are digital, perhaps you could email them to me.

I look forward to hearing from you and perhaps coming to tell you more about David's book.

Yours sincerely

Following up the background

The benefit of a Life or Child Appreciation Day is that it should provide a wealth of information. If it is not possible to hold one, then the child's social worker should visit significant people in the child's life to gather further information to help to form as complete a picture as possible. These people may include the birth parents and wider family, residential unit staff and former foster carers. Again, you will need to write first to let them know the purpose of your visit. Do not forget to include support workers and other people who tried to help the birth family stay together.

Birth parents and their extended family

Do not be afraid to approach birth parents, even if it is a long time since they saw their child. Don't ask just once – it can take several times over a period of time before the parent agrees. Those involved with a child are usually anxious about this. They may say, 'She has forgotten her mother…Why stir up the past? It will only push her mother into making trouble…' Such worries are genuine. Obviously a birth parent should not be approached if this might cause harm to the child, but be sure of your own motivation if you decide not to ask for the birth parents' help. Is it to protect the child or to protect yourself?

When we first started to approach birth parents, we were worried about the damage we might cause. Perhaps we have been lucky, but we have never ceased to be amazed by birth parents' willingness to co-operate; making clear why the information is needed encourages the co-operation.

Usually it is only the birth family that can provide the information to make a family tree, one of the best ways of showing a child where he or she "came from", which we discuss later.

Often, in cases where a child's parents were not married, the birth mother will provide information about the birth father. Perhaps it will be the first time she has been asked about him in a way that seems relevant to her. She might reveal such insights for the child as 'He had blue eyes', or 'He was six foot tall', or 'He loved the countryside', or 'He was good with animals'. It is unlikely that in her contact with officials, she will ever have been asked for this kind of information. A birth parent is usually reticent to provide information for fear of it being used as evidence in court against them so it may be necessary to wait until any court proceedings are over.

Where the father of a child is not known, there may have been good reason for the birth mother to have concealed his identity. The number of children born as a consequence of incest is very difficult to assess, but there are certain patterns of sexual abuse within families that could suggest that a child may be the product of incest. It may, of course, be known and be documented on the child's file. Such information will need to be handled very sensitively for the child. It is important, therefore, not to assume that the context in which a child was conceived was necessarily one of a loving relationship. Having a child as a result of incest can have negative consequences in terms of the birth mother's parenting abilities. This would be important to convey to the child – that the birth mother was perhaps constantly reminded of things she wished to forget whenever the child was around – and would need to be handled sensitively.

The birth mother might also provide an account of her own childhood. This can often help her child to understand and come to terms with being unable to live with her. Sometimes the child will learn that one parent has either been separated from their original family or had an unhappy childhood. It can be good to know how the parents met, what they were good at school, whether they were naughty, etc. How did they feel when the baby was on its way, what hopes did they have for it, why did they choose the name, and so on.

Parents with learning disability may need extra support to be able to deal with the interview and communicate.

Residential centre staff

Some children will have lived in several residential centres. Staff, especially cooks, cleaners and gardeners, who have worked in an establishment or centre for a long time, will have photographs that you can borrow. These may be of the child in a group, or of the staff or of the centre itself.

Foster carers

Foster families will often have photographs of the children they have fostered; they are also a source of information and anecdotes to draw upon in life story work. Many will have memory boxes of memorabilia from the child's time with them (which is an expectation of the Minimum Fostering Standards, Standard 26.7).

Be prepared to exercise imagination and flair in obtaining photographs, treasures, school work, old toys – anything that helps children to understand that they have a past and gives them a sense of identity and belonging.

4 Getting started

There is no set procedure for life story work. The approach we take may not be suitable for you, and you will discover your own approach or you may want to consider Joy Rees' (2009) suggestion that you start the work in the present before moving to the past and then the future. Remember, too, that the goal is not necessarily to produce a book, video or product; the process and journey you undertake with the child are important. You may be documenting sessions in different ways, but whatever is produced will belong to the child. Avoid jargon and keep sentences simple. If you are guided by the child or they write it themselves, this should happen naturally. For older children, using digital technology will be more appropriate, and this is discussed more fully in Chapter 14.

Rapport building

The most important first step when starting your contact with the child is to build rapport. If this has not been achieved, say at a previous meeting with the child, then you will need to pay special attention to it now. Basically, you need to establish a trusting and comfortable way of being with and talking to the child. This is not wasted time since it helps the child to be able to talk to you, especially about uncomfortable issues. This may mean playing with the child, going on a day trip or to the cinema, or any other leisure activity such as electronic games. You and the child will have the chance to start talking to each other about unimportant and everyday issues and to explore any anxieties the child may have about meeting with you on a regular basis. You may need to re-establish rapport from time to time – the child should feel comfortable about being with you and the activities you share. This is an important part of your work.

Positive attending

We have been particularly impressed by a training course recently published by BAAF (now CoramBAAF), titled *Fostering Changes: How to improve relationships and manage behaviour* (Pallett *et al*, 2011).

A section titled "Positive Attention" (pp147–155) is, we feel, especially useful when applied to how we consider building rapport, and we reproduce some extracts below.

Attending

...has evolved through the work of such clinicians as McMahon and Forehand and Webster-Stratton. "Attending" involves carers in using their attention to encourage and reward appropriate behaviour. This brings about improvements in the relationship between the child and carer as well as increased levels of compliance and self-esteem in the child.

Play

One of the most straightforward ways of providing positive attention to children under the age of 12 is through the medium of play. Play enables children to learn about themselves and the world around them. It offers opportunities for the development of a range of skills, from physical co-ordination to creative, linguistic and cognitive skills. It also provides a means for the child to learn about and explore a host of social situations and to develop skills like taking turns, empathy, and co-operation...Skills in attending will enable carers to provide affirming, supportive and non-intrusive attention through play. These positive experiences of play can be very rewarding and create an enduring sense of fun, warmth and intimacy.

Listening as attending

Attending skills can be used to tune in to what a child is saying, both at a verbal and non-verbal level and to gently reflect back what you understand them to have said. With younger children, and those who experience difficulty in understanding or expressing their feelings, carers may need to actually acknowledge and name the child's feelings. Children need to learn the vocabulary of feelings in much the same way that they learn to name objects. The carer might say something like, 'it seems to me that you feel sad because Pete can't come and play' or 'sounds like you're angry with me for insisting you do your homework first'. Instead of quizzing the child about what they feel, the carer can get alongside them and comment on what they observe. Like play attending, this kind of listening is non-intrusive and responds to the child's cues and lead. This needs to be done with sensitivity, as carers will not necessarily always interpret the child's emotional state accurately.

Tips on attending

The tips on "attending" are particularly useful, and are reproduced below.

- Follow your child's lead.

- Go at your child's pace.

- Sit close.

- Don't compete.

- Praise and encourage your child's ideas and creativity.

- Use descriptive comments instead of questions.

- Reward quiet play with your attention.

- Be an appreciative audience, don't take over.

- Get involved in your child's make-believe play.

- Ignore inappropriate behaviour.

- Encourage the child to do his/her own problem-solving.

- Laugh and have fun.

- Give a warning before you are going to finish.

- Reward yourself for your efforts and successes!

(Pallett *et al*, 2011, p171)

Starting the session

Each session should focus on the task of getting to know the child in order to make progress with the life story work. This means – and we repeat this because it is so important – that you become a regular, reliable and predictable person in the child's life. Make appointments and keep them, and turn up on time! If you cannot, speak to the child yourself on the phone and don't leave messages if you can help it.

David, whose life story book is occasionally used to illustrate this guide, obviously thought that adults were untrustworthy and unreliable. He said at our eighth meeting, 'You always come on the day you say you will, don't you?'

How long should a session last?

The length of a session will depend on a number of factors: whether the child lives with you, the child's span of concentration, the time you have available. Ideally, you should set a specific time for each session. We find that an hour is perhaps the maximum time we can hold our own concentration, and, for this reason, we usually structure the session to last roughly that long.

If the child lives with you, perhaps the weekend is the best time for these sessions because both of you may be more relaxed and free from weekday pressures.

How often will you meet?

Kay Donley, in her "Ten Commandments", states that you should become a regular and consistent person in your child's life. What is meant by "regular"? We feel that in the early stages, say the first eight to ten weeks of working with a child, you should aim for weekly sessions. However, you may find that once a fortnight, though less satisfactory, is more realistic. Try to avoid raising your child's expectations by frequent contact in the first three or four weeks and then becoming erratic in your later contact.

Surprisingly, if you are either a residential social worker, foster carer or adoptive parent and the child lives with you, it can be difficult to arrange regular sessions. It is often a problem to find a mutually convenient time within the domestic and social rhythms of the household. A person outside of the household can interrupt these rhythms more easily. A foster carer's free time can clash with a child's time, for example, when he or she either wants to watch television or play with friends.

The most important aim is that the life story work is started and the sessions are consistent. It may seem a big commitment and this could deter you. Vera Fahlberg, a psychotherapist with considerable experience of working with children and families who have experienced difficulties, states that 'tomorrow is made harder by lack of preparation today'. In other words, this is time well spent and may eventually save you time by helping to ensure that your child's placement does not break down and will help if contact is made through social media.

What materials do you need?

If you are producing a book, all you need, apart from the photographs and other documents, is a loose-leaf folder and paper, and it is useful to have pens, coloured pencils and glue handy for drawing, writing and putting pictures into the folder. A loose-leaf folder allows you to make corrections and to add new material as it comes to light.

Alternatively, you could use a pre-prepared book titled *My Life and Me* (Camis, 2001), which is a colourful spiral-bound life story workbook, divided into colour-coded sections, with space for drawings, photographs and documents, for children to use; practice guidelines are included that will help social workers and carers to understand the significance of completing each of the sections.

Children who are looked after often experience learning difficulties and it is important that they are not made to struggle with writing. You can help them with spelling, if requested, but avoid correcting any mistakes. Some children enjoy dictating for you to write or type, or you could write in pencil for the child to go over in ink. Always remember that this is the child's own private book, not a showpiece. Be prepared for it to be somewhat untidy and messy and allow the child to include anything he or she wants.

If you are producing a video, DVD or CD or memory stick, apart from having a way of recording, you will need to arrange to film relevant material, including significant people and places. Children could actively participate by also doing some of the filming themselves. You may also need to gather together objects that have had significance for the child, including toys, mementos, birthday cards, photographs of family members, etc, so that you can weave them into your film. If you are using a computer-aided package, for example, *My Life Story* (Betts and Ahmad, 2003), you will need a computer on which you can run the programme and a safe place to keep the CD-ROM.

Of course, there are still other ways in which life story work could be tackled, for example, using wallpaper to create a wall chart, or using a box of some kind to keep together important mementos, or drawing maps, family trees, or family circles, or doing it digitally, of which more later.

Surrey Children's Services have, as part of their commitment to life story work, put together a life story work e-learning resources platform, that social workers, family support workers, foster carers and adopters are able to access. The intention was to create a colourful, user-friendly central platform that would be available to everyone; not intended to replace training, but to provide a range of useful materials and guidance, including podcasts by young people and carers, printable activity sheets and resources, details of relevant books to use with children, quick guides and policy documents. The platform is accessible from laptops, tablets and smartphones to make it as versatile as possible.

Who else should be involved?

You need to work away from distractions and interruptions. However, it is important to have another adult involved in the work, although not part of the session. For example, if you are a foster carer, the child's social worker will have to provide most of the factual information and seek out photographs. As the work progresses, the child might wish to show and talk about the life story to this significant adult, who has helped in this way. Doing so may help you to ascertain how the child is absorbing and understanding the past. As the project progresses, members of the birth family may also be regularly involved.

Who keeps the life story work?

Without question, the life story work belongs to the child. Should he or she, therefore, be allowed to keep it? Of course, but the timing is important. Some would argue that, as the book belongs to the child, he or she should always keep it. This is the ideal and should certainly be what happens towards the end of the time you are working together. However, at certain stages some children destroy their life story work if it is in their possession. The child may be overwhelmed by a sense of anger and frustration about what has happened and may direct this at the work. It used to be that valuable photographs and documents were lost forever but using scanners, digital photos and placing them in a computer folder safeguards against this. In the early stages, therefore, we recommend that you are prudent and make sure that the book, film , CD-ROM or encrypted memory stick is kept in a safe place. Remember to back up material on a computer. At all times the child should have reasonable access to it, but this needs to be supervised.

Our "hard" and main copy is a ring binder, so that children can edit bits in or out and have a physical means of access to their information (a readily available printed photo could be worth 10 or 20 photographs in an electronic folder). For example, a child's emotional response to a particular adult in their life may be affected by current issues that they are discussing. This is especially relevant for children who have been sexually assaulted and have not disclosed this at the time of their life story work. There may be a picture of them with the perpetrator in their book. Whilst the child may at some point in the future like to reclaim positive feelings they had for their parent who sexually offended against them, it may be that at this point they are unable to experience positive feelings.

You may decide to provide a photo album separately (even if it is stored digitally on a computer), and this alleviates the problem of how to keep the book safely and yet share it with your child. Administrative convenience, "hot desk" working and paperless storage systems that involve destroying paper files, means that a letter from a birth parent exists only in a scanned form. The magic of a photo or letter written perhaps fifty years earlier is a wonder to behold.

Usually we find that the best time to give the book, or whatever else is produced, into a child's own keeping is when the child has joined the new family and is showing signs of being secure with them. It may well become a proud possession that the child wants to show to others and turn to occasionally. A social worker in Northern Ireland comments in *Life Books for Children in Care* (Northern Ireland Foster Care Association, 1995):

> *Through their life books, our children have come to own their own story little by little, mainly because they have gone through them so often with other people and each time it becomes clearer to them. Besides, in retelling it, they think of new questions to ask and gain new realisations each time.*

Who can look at the life story work?

The answer is no one – without the child's permission. This, of course, is another element of confidentiality. Nonetheless, encouraging the child to share the product of his or her life story work should be a feature of your work. For example, foster carers might suggest that their child talk about the book with their social worker. If the child agrees, it can provide an opportunity to talk about events in their life. An additional bonus can be that the person who is helping the child make the book can gauge the level of understanding from the way their child talks about the past. But you must be sure that the child really wants to share the book and is not just agreeing to please you.

It is implicit from the beginning of doing life story work, where the plan is to place a child in a new family, that the new family will be shown whatever is produced. This is made easier because we always include the child's anxieties and aspirations for the future in life story work, for example, the child's desire to own a bicycle or to remain in contact with someone from the past. One girl, worried about how she might be punished by her new parents, wrote in her book, 'It is alright to be smacked, but not to be hit with a belt'. A four-year-old had written for him, 'I wish I was two years old again'; in response to being asked why, he said it was because his mummy and daddy still lived together then. Through life story work, children can have a safe way of making known their expectations to their new family, and perhaps to offer past experiences to talk about.

We have found that, as they move towards placement, many children allow their prospective family to look at their book or work. From the other side, we encourage the prospective families to make their own life story book for the child to see. Children appreciate this gesture and it can be a very good "ice breaker". *My Life and Me* (Camis, 2001) is a colourful life story workbook which includes space for drawings, photographs, and words to record thoughts and feelings at various stages in a child's life (see Further Reading).

How will the work affect you?

As we have said before, you should never betray the child's confidence and should not avoid talking about the things the child wants to talk about because they make you feel uncomfortable.

Most of us have also experienced feelings of loss and separation. Working with children who are unravelling their own sufferings may release some of these feelings within ourselves. It is important that you have help and support from someone you can talk to about what is happening to you. If you are a foster carer, your local foster carer group may be able to help. Some of these groups hold regular meetings for foster carers who are helping their children with life story work. Other people may turn to the child's social worker for support, and social workers, in turn, to their colleagues for support or their managers for supervision.

What problems will you face?

In taking on life story work, you can expect some regression from the child as a matter of course. By "regression" we mean a return to behaviour that might have been left behind, or taking on behaviour patterns that belong to a much younger age group. A common experience, for example, is that the child's behaviour will go back to that appropriate for the age at which they were first separated from their family.

Everyone has their own way of dealing with these problems. However, regressive behaviour will not persist and we have never taken it as a sign that we should discontinue life story work. If children find life story work too threatening, they simply will not do it and will make it quite clear to you, not simply regress for a period (we discuss regression further in the next chapter).

Be honest, but not brutal

Every child is hurt by separation from their family. Use this knowledge in talking to the child. Many of the other adults in a child's life may tell you that he or she is completely untouched by it and never wants to talk about it. You must know better, and work to allow the child to express this hurt and anger at some stage. They will want to do this, but may never have found anyone who has been trustworthy enough to tell. You may be the first person who has gained their trust in being consistent in wanting to know all about them.

Don't impose your version of events on the child, as many adults will have done. You want to find out what the child thinks about what has happened. If you disagree with what you think is fantasy, say so, but be no more authoritative than you would be in disagreeing with another adult.

It may be helpful for you to tell the child what you think may have happened, particularly if there are indicators of undisclosed abuse in the family of origin. It may be that the abuse is clearly documented in the social work file, but the child appears not to remember. Acknowledging how awful life has been in their family of origin may be an important step for traumatised children to move forward in their lives and begin the process of recovery.

Be honest, but not brutal. If you cover up or prevaricate, the child will know it and will not trust you as much. If you side with children in running down their parents or others, you will find later that they will not be honest with you when talking about their past or their feelings about others. Try to identify some positive features about people they complain about, but don't cover up the negatives. Try to be even-handed and objective about why people do things and children will trust you more than if you join in a tirade against their family and friends. Remember that their birth family is part of them; criticising the family will eventually feel like criticism of them. Birth families continue to live in children's hearts and minds, even when they are not physically present. This became apparent in the "Contact After Adoption" study (Neil *et al*, 2015).

Finally, remember that every child is an individual with a very interesting story to tell if you can help them to do it. Let them know that you are interested and can be trusted and eventually they will want to tell you all about themselves.

5 Some questions answered

We have made it clear throughout that life story work with a child can be fraught with difficulties. If you are aware of some of these difficulties, you will be more able to face them together should you meet them. We pose here some of the frequently asked questions.

My child was seriously injured as a toddler. How do I explain that?

We are frequently asked how you tell a child potentially unpleasant things about his or her parents. It is easier to answer this by giving some examples of what you should **not** say:

> *Your birth mother loved you very much, but she did not have enough money to look after you because she had no job.*

What happens then if either wage earner in a new family is made redundant? And how do you explain birth parents who are now working?

> *Your first mummy became ill, and that is why you came to live with us. But she still loves you.*

What happens then when either you become ill or the birth mother gets better?

What may appear to be an act of kindness to protect the child is often an excuse to avoid a painful issue by the adult involved. The motto "knowledge dispels fear" comes from a parachute school, but it is transferable to assisting a child to understand the past.

A child growing up in the love and security of a family would normally have knowledge and understanding of most of the events in that family's life. Not to have such information and knowledge can lead to confusion, unhappiness, and misery. Often a child will blame themselves for unhappy events in their past. Part of a child's coping strategy is a sense of loyalty and a defence of their family. It is unlikely that they will easily be able to let go until they feel safe and supported to do so.

There is often a very real sense of void. Some children have talked about a "physical emptiness", others about a "knot" inside them. Knowledge can fill a void; understanding can dispel what is often an irrational fear and untie the knot. We know from adults who have been adopted as babies that to stumble upon the knowledge of their adoption in later life can have a devastating effect. The very foundation that their lives are built on can suddenly turn to sand. It is better to face reality gradually as a child and come to terms with it.

When your problem is how to explain why your child was harmed, there is no easy solution, but lying about it will not help. With the younger child, you need give little detail in the early stages, but gradually provide more detail in response to questions as the child gets older. Children often ask what they want to know, not what you want to tell them. Listen to the questions carefully and answer what the child has asked – the information given should be "age-appropriate".

DAVID

David had been removed from his mother's care because it was considered that she had neglected him. Yet she was neither bad nor wicked, more a victim of circumstances. Before we talked to David about this, we had obtained a family tree from her. From this, her own unhappy childhood came to light. She talked about struggling alone with David in a bed-sitter, a 17-year-old with no help and little money.

Once we understood this, we talked together as a team about how we should explain events to David. This is what we told him:

> *Mary, your birth mum, had an unhappy childhood; she spent some time in a residential unit herself. When you were born, she lived with her mother for a while, but decided to try to live in a bed-sitter with you. She was all on her own without any help. Sometimes, because she was lonely, she went out and left you on your own. At other times, when you cried, as all young children do, she smacked you too hard and bruised you. She was not a bad person, but did not know how to look after young children. She wanted to be a good parent but did not succeed.*

The person undertaking life story work needs to guard against a tendency to assure children they were loved when the evidence points to the opposite of this. Children may have experienced physical and sexual abuse, going hungry and living in fear. It may be appropriate to say their parent was not able to be a good parent.

How do I explain that a sibling remains at home?

Situations change and it may not be a reflection on your child that they are not with their birth family but a comment on the ability of the birth parents to care for children of different ages or gender. Most children can understand that it is easier to look after a baby than a troubled and challenging six-year-old. There is no need to avoid the issue of your child being difficult to look after, this needs to be discussed and resolved anyway.

What do I do if the child wants to put something untrue in the book?

You should not put untrue things in the book. This is an opportunity to discuss why they want to do this and see if they are remembering false events or just want to change reality so it hurts less. If the child persists, suggest you can agree to disagree and will come back to that later.

If children know that they can ask questions about the past freely throughout their childhood, you will have removed a major source of potential difficulty. The past will no longer be a mystery, not to be discussed. You will have demystified it and made it normal, everyday and ordinary.

Children who have suffered many separations will blame themselves and believe that they are bad. If their parents were "bad", it must mean they have inherited this "badness"; they may even believe they were the cause of their parents' "badness". If you can help your child to understand the events and circumstances of the past, this will go a long way to healing the deep wounds of the hurt that has been suffered.

What if my child begins to lose interest in life story work?

From time to time during life story work, the child's interest will wane. Our descriptive illustrations in this book are only "edited highlights". We have spent many sessions when little progress seems to have been made. This need not be a problem.

There will be periods when nothing much is said or done during your sessions. If you are arriving at the same time each week or fortnight, you will have little control over what mood the child is in. If you force the pace, the life story work will become unpleasant for the child and that is not what you want. Of course, if the child is living with you, it is possible to choose moments to work together when the child wishes to respond, but even so, there may be periods when the work is very slow.

All the time that you are helping a child, you need someone with whom to discuss events, and this is especially necessary when you are in the doldrums. There are some play techniques you can introduce after discussion with the colleagues and friends who are providing you with support.

What if my child regresses?

We have said already that during life story work, the child's behaviour may regress to that of a younger child. You should be prepared for this. Regression can take a whole range and variety of forms. Bed-wetting and soiling, temper tantrums, becoming quiet and withdrawn are just a few.

One 12-year-old boy insisted on being carried to bed each evening. Gradually this changed to being "chased" to bed and, eventually, he went to bed normally. During this period he also presented problems at school: shouting out in class, scribbling in his exercise books whenever his work was criticised. His foster carers regarded his developmental age at this period as being that of a six-year-old.

This regression is to be expected. It is a normal reaction. The movement backwards is usually short-lived and from it comes a healthy growth. It is important to know that your child may regress and that you may need help through difficult patches from other foster carers/adopters or your social worker, if you are the foster carer/adopter, or from colleagues if you are the worker involved.

6 Helping the child to talk about feelings

You will find as you work that the child will dictate the pace. Some of what is revealed will be distressing to both of you. If you are at a loss as to how to respond to this distress in words, physical affection or a sympathetic smile helps children to feel that you are on their side and are not put off by them or their past.

We have found that it is necessary from the beginning to establish that you are aware that the child has good/bad, happy/sad, and positive/ negative feelings, and it is vital to establish that the child is aware that it is safe to talk about the bad as well as the good.

There are approaches that we have found useful in demonstrating that you accept these opposite emotions. Try to make it interesting and even enjoyable for children to express themselves by getting them to make things and draw pictures. We describe here how we have worked through pictures to help children to talk about feelings in a way that is safe for them. Violet Oaklander in her book, *Windows to our Children*, suggests and explains many useful ideas that can help children to express these emotions (see Further Reading). Two picture books for children, *Morris and the Bundle of Worries* (Seeney, 2008), and *Elfa and the Box of Memories* (Bell, 2008), will help children talk about their feelings, anxieties and memories.

Some workers use stories to help the child to open up. Stories can help the child identify with a character and their experiences and prompt him or her to talk about this as well as their own, and realise that other children might have had similar feelings/experiences, and thus feel enabled to talk more directly about their own experiences.

> I like my *friends*
>
> I hate it when **I don't have anyone to play with.**
>
> I am afraid to **Go out in the dark on my own**
>
> My face has a big smile when **I'm doing something fun**
>
> I hate to eat **Cucumber**
>
> I hope that **I'll get a bike for my Birthday**

Using questionnaires

A questionnaire is a set of questions or unfinished sentences, like those shown in this illustration, which the child can answer, react to and discuss. A questionnaire can be useful in several ways in the early stages of working with a child on a life story.

Because of the structured nature of questionnaires, less demand is made on the child to be forthcoming and inventive. It is therefore particularly useful for children not used to writing down their thoughts or whose literacy is limited. For these children and for those who find it difficult to express themselves, for whatever reason, the questionnaire method can be used as a lead-in to producing a life story book or video, and could be included in the front of a life story book.

The structure of questionnaires is a matter of your choice, and you can buy questionnaire booklets (see Further Reading). Some of these are simply lists of questions progressing in sensitivity from fairly neutral questions, such as:

What is your favourite colour?

Which colour don't you like?

to more sensitive questions, such as:

Who is your favourite person?

Who is your least favourite person?

Which person do you dislike most?

These questions lead children into making statements about themselves. They get them used to expressing both negative and positive statements about themselves and also convey the message that you are interested in their thoughts and feelings.

Some questionnaire books are structured differently and allow more creativity, like *My Life and Me* (Camis, 2001). They may contain, for example, a blank page with the heading, 'This is a picture of my favourite person' or 'This is how I see myself', thus encouraging children to draw pictures expressing aspects of themselves or their hopes and fears.

You can construct your own questionnaire encouraging the child to illustrate the cover with photos, drawings, elaborate writing or stick-on paper shapes. If you construct a questionnaire booklet yourself, you can make it lead into areas that will be helpful for the child. One obvious idea is to omit negative statements altogether if you are working with a child who seems to have a wholly negative image of him or herself. Thus the questionnaire booklet when completed will contain only positive statements about the child.

Questionnaires can be structured to help a child to think about the future, with questions such as:

When I grow up I will live in...

When I leave this residential unit I will feel...

When I go to a new family, it will help me to...

The possibilities are endless. Don't forget, however, that questionnaires are only a method of eliciting information. They are not a substitute for life story work, which allows freer discussion and a wider-ranging expression of views than questionnaires do by themselves.

In using questionnaires we avoid trying to interpret the answers back to the child. The answers to some questions may be very significant, or appear so, but to go into them in depth at an early stage would unsettle some children and might warn them off opening up and revealing their inner and private world. In other words, don't push too early.

Using pictures to enable a child to talk about feelings

Invite the child to draw a picture of him/herself and the things they like best that make them happy. Encourage them to write a caption to the picture about these happy/enjoyable events or to dictate such a caption for you to write. Try not to lead them or to search for any hidden meaning. Keep the activity simple and reproduce the child's own words.

Once this is completed to the child's satisfaction, suggest that he or she draws a picture of something they hate to do or which makes them angry. Usually children deny that anything makes them angry or sad, or that there is anything they hate. Often it has not been safe to show these feelings, so to deny them is normal. Don't push this issue.

Some children will respond with "safe" dislikes. A six-year-old girl wrote 'I do not like those yellow things at school'. We later found that she meant the sweetcorn occasionally served with school dinners. You might encourage a listing of "safe" things that are hated, like cabbage, plums or 'those yellow things'.

All that you are doing at this stage is showing that you are aware that the child has both positive and negative feelings and that you accept both

things I like

things I don't like

unconditionally. Sometimes there is resistance to drawing pictures, but we have successfully "broken the ice" with the questionnaire method and the happy/sad face.

There will be some children totally cut off from their feelings – disassociated; these children may need some preparatory work in using their senses, for example, asking the child to recognise and describe taste, textures, sounds, etc, in order to feel safe enough to move on to exploring feelings.

The happy/sad face

This face is made from two paper plates. One of them is cut in half and hinged to the back of the other so that it can be alternated.

The child – or you – can draw a happy face on the full plate. Then the half plate is turned over and either a sad or an angry face drawn on it. With this it is then possible to ask, 'Who are you today? Are you Miss Happy or Miss Sad?'

We have taken this further by asking the child to describe how "the face" might be feeling inside. If the child can do this, we write their comments

on the "feelings" cards (see following page). You should avoid rushing this stage, especially if it is early on in your work with the child.

"Feelings" cards

In order to express emotions, children need a repertoire of words that they feel comfortable using. Providing words to describe these feelings can be difficult, for the child will resist acknowledging that such emotions exist. Vera Fahlberg, in her film *Adoptive Children, Adaptive Feelings*, demonstrates a technique she has developed – the use of "feelings" cards. These are a set of cards each of which has a single word that identifies a specific emotional response.

We have taken this idea and used it with an individual child and with groups of children by making the initial introduction of these words into a game. The child (or children) is encouraged to call out words that describe an emotion and these words are written onto blank cards. The words may be, for example, good, bad, happy, sad, miserable, cheerful, kind, cruel. Once sufficient words have been gathered, the game continues with the child drawing a face to match each "feelings" word (see illustration).

This is a helpful exercise because it familiarises children with emotive words and gradually sensitises them to using these words to describe their feelings about situations and events. Introduced in this way, the potential threat and danger children may experience, when attempts are made to attribute such feelings to them, are avoided.

For example, when you are later talking about an incident in the child's past, the cards can be laid out and the child can be encouraged to pick out a card that describes how they felt at the time. This method could be used when a child is describing how they felt at leaving a particular foster home and perhaps how they feel about it now. In this way, past trauma can often be gradually resolved.

Throughout your work together, you can refer back to the cards from time to time and ask the child to add more words. A useful word is "upset". It covers a range of emotions and can be a substitute for a stronger emotion, such as "angry" which the child may not be ready to use, especially in the early stages.

What will the child get from these sessions?

Don't be worried by what appears to be a lack of emotional response at this stage. Drawing the good/bad pictures has an impact that will not become apparent until much later in life story work.

Avoid interpreting any of the drawings, and accept a child's statement that they cannot think of anything that makes them upset. If they do disclose a small portion of their inner world, let it pass at this meeting, but make a note of it to be used as a reference point later. For example, when a child is starting to discuss feelings of loss, you might say, 'Do you remember when you drew a happy picture and could think of nothing that made you upset? I think that you feel upset because Anne lives with Mary, your "born to" mother, and you do not.'

7 Some elements of a life story book

If you are making a life story book as part of the work, there are various elements that may be included. We list some of them here and then go on to discuss them in detail.

Where I came from
My birth certificate
My family tree
Photographs about me

My life graph
Visiting the past
My own map

We illustrate how these elements work with some examples from the life story book of "David" that he made with one of us some years ago when he was eight.

Where I came from

We used to assume that most children knew where babies come from. Now we know that this is not the case, and you will have to discover how much your child actually knows before you talk about this. Mother-and-baby books and health education books from your local health centre or library should provide all the visual aids necessary to cover the period from conception to the first birthday, or you can look for age-appropriate information online.

David was, fortunately, aware that a baby grows in its mother's tummy, and from there it was a simple step to establish that he started to grow in Mary's (his birth mother) tummy when John planted his seed.

pregnant mum

At this early stage, because photographs from relatives, foster carers and others may be slow to arrive, you will have to improvise, returning to fill in details later.

The hospital where the child was born will provide the time of birth and the weight at birth. You can give this information direct to the older child, but a younger child needs to be helped to understand it. The child can draw a clock face showing the time of birth and can stick in the book the equivalent of the birth weight in, say, pictures of bags of sugar.

The child can draw or collect pictures of very young children and give them captions. For example:

> *This is my drawing of a baby at six months.*
> *I might have looked like this.*

> *I had my first birthday party at Oak Street where I lived with John and Mary, my born-to dad and mum.*

My birth certificate

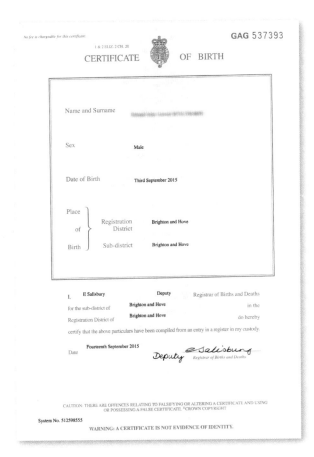

When we first started to do life story work with children, we provided a photocopy of their birth certificate to complete the part about their birth; we thought it would only be of passing interest to them. We were not prepared for the potent effect it had. Now we find it usually occupies a whole session. It can be of immense interest to the child and can provoke numerous questions. Even small children who cannot read seem to grasp its significance, that it is documentary evidence that they were born and have an identity, which can never be taken away from them. At the same time, the birth certificate can have a temporarily unsettling effect on adoptive parents and foster carers. For them, it is also documentary evidence that they are not the "born to" parents of their child. If you are in this position, remember that there is more to being a parent than giving birth and it is only if you are able to accept the facts of your child's birth that the child will feel accepted by you as his or her new parents.

Who's who

It is recognised now that the permanent, stable nuclear family is not the only family structure into which children are born and grow up. Whatever the arguments for and against this are, it certainly has the result that children have many more complex relationships to understand and adjust to than was once the case. It is not unusual for the family group to have siblings where the blood ties are only through one parent.

We need to remember that family structures do not remain static and that when a child leaves his or her family of origin, the parents may enter into new relationships where new partners bring with them their children. Further children may also be born into the new relationship so that the separated child acquires new half-siblings. Not unnaturally, these situations may confuse the child with whom you are working and arouse feelings of envy or resentment towards those siblings who have stayed, or been born into, the family of origin.

It is often helpful to explore these feelings in a group setting, where all the children have similar backgrounds (see also Chapter 11, *Working with groups*). This helps a child to understand that their family situation is not abnormal, and that their feelings and possible confusions are shared by other children in similar situations.

Today, social work practice recognises the importance of working in partnership with people who have played a significant role in a child's life; this is enshrined in legislation in the UK. Similarly, moves towards open adoption signal a greater understanding of adoption as a life-long process, where adopted people need to know and understand their origins, and may work to maintain links with their birth family. It is important for a child to understand the nature of their relationship with all the people in their family of origin and for this they require reliable information, especially for the future, when they need to keep themselves safe.

In our counselling of adults who were adopted as children, we have been faced time and time again with the anger and hurt that can result from an adult discovering that they have brothers and sisters whose existence they were not aware of whilst they were children.

Ecomaps, family trees and diagrams of blood ties have all proved useful as ways of explaining a child's relationship to siblings, half-siblings and significant adults in their family of origin.

We live in an era in which four in ten marriages end in divorce (statistic from Gingerbread, a charity for single parents). Many people enter into relationships that are stable and in which they have children. Some of these relationships eventually end too. As the years progress, there may be a tangled network of full siblings, half-siblings and stepsiblings. It should be remembered that these family networks are neither abnormal nor unusual and it is important for children to understand this. We have found that looking at the complexity of family ties can be usefully incorporated when working with children in groups. In doing so, children can become aware that, although their lives are unique, there are similarities with the experiences of other children. Legislation emphasises the importance of family links, regrettably all too frequently ignored in the past. For example, if David's father and paternal grandparents had been approached at the time he was removed from his birth mother's care, perhaps his life would have run a different course.

We have developed the following illustration from our work with children to help them, and us, understand how the family network has emerged and how the blood ties developed. Although we have attempted to keep this illustration very simple, it demonstrates that family ties quickly become complicated and difficult to understand once they break the commonly-perceived mould of a married couple with two children. It is worth repeating that this concept of family life, regularly portrayed in the media, particularly on television, is not the norm and the model drawn here is perhaps closer to reality than most of us realise.

WAYNE

Sharon and Kevin met when they were 17 years old.

Sharon became pregnant and gave birth to Wayne. Kevin was Wayne's father. Kevin said he was too young to marry and he and Sharon drifted apart. Sharon often visited Kevin's mother (Wayne's grandmother) with Wayne.

When Wayne was two years old, Sharon met Pete and they started to go out together.

Pete had lived with Alison for five years and they had two children, Annie and Cheryl. Pete and Alison had stopped living together about six months before Pete met Sharon.

Pete and Sharon married in May 2010. Pete became Wayne's stepfather.

Pete and Mary had two children, Lisa and Alan.

Sharon told Wayne that Lisa and Alan were his "half" brother and sister.

Annie and Cheryl were Lisa and Alan's half-sisters and Wayne's stepsisters.

Meanwhile, Kevin, Wayne's father, had married Maria and had two children, Carla and Amanda. Wayne used to see his half-siblings at his grandparents' (Kevin's parents).

On the following page we show what the family links would look like.

The colours, and the way in which they blend, are used to identify the blood ties. Children may need assurance that they did not have to have a "blood tie" to a significant adult to be loved. Sadly, for Wayne, it was used to help him understand why Pete treated him differently and eventually rejected him.

Understanding these family links and ties is essential for the child to understand their place in the family network and in future contact arrangements, if and where appropriate. It is through helping the child understand these relationships, talking to the child and establishing what

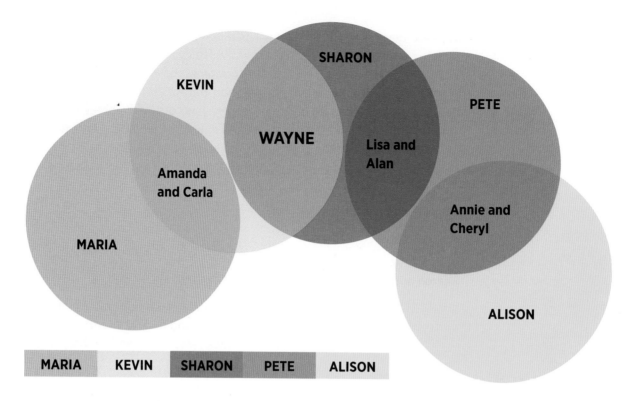

is significant for the child, that we will be able to engage the child in decisions about contact.

In the past, when parental contact with the child has been terminated, this has almost automatically included siblings, grandparents and other significant adults, such as aunts and uncles. Evidence from counselling adults who had been separated from siblings in childhood suggests that they feel robbed of these childhood experiences.

Planning for children requires a comprehensive assessment. Using the "family ties graph", the family tree graph and the life graph can be an important element in such an assessment. Legislation states clearly that children are best cared for in their own families. If, on completing all this work, it is not possible for the child to be cared for in his or her own family, then this work can be used as a basis for understanding why this is not possible.

My family tree

As we have said, the birth family is the best source of information for making a family tree. We consider that its making, and showing the child his or her place on it, is very important. Knowledge of the extended family can be painful to children because it emphasises that they are severed from their birth family and forebears. Nonetheless, it can also do a great deal to help children understand some of the events that led to the loss of their family.

By working on his family tree, Jimmy, a nine-year-old, could start to understand why he came to be looked after as a two-year-old, bruised and neglected. He understood that his mother was 16 years old when he was born, and that she too had been "in care".

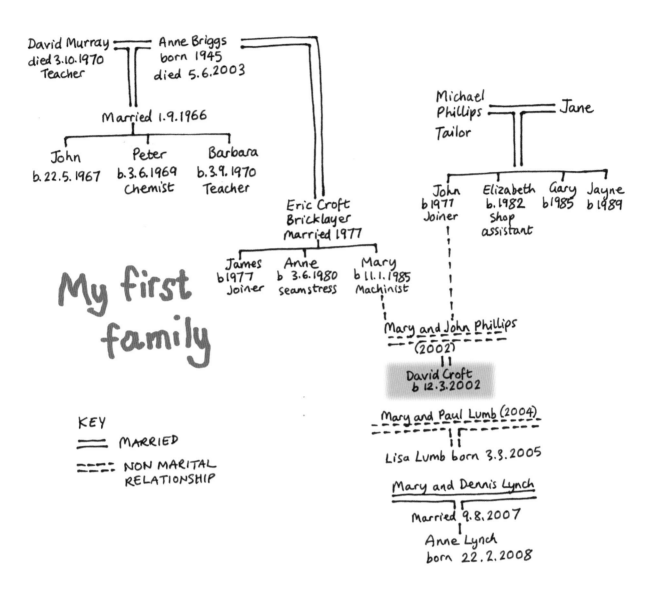

My first family

KEY
═══ MARRIED
═══ NON MARITAL RELATIONSHIP

Jimmy was living in a large residential unit in which there were several 16-year-old girls. He began to grasp that his mother was not bad or cruel, just very young and ill-prepared to be a mother to him.

Remember that family patterns are now diverse and it may help children to accept their own situations to know that there are such variations. Four marriages in ten end in divorce and one child in four lives in a single parent family. Life story work should not, therefore, attempt to portray a model of family life that is alien to the child and removed from the diverse family structures that exist in society.

Frequently, children come from such changing households with further developments occurring after they have left. These complicated relationships can be an additional source of stress for a child because the changes are difficult to understand.

If the plans are to resettle children back in their birth families, it is important to ensure that they have a knowledge and understanding of the changes that have gone on since they left. If the child is not returning to the birth family, and the changes in the family are one of the reasons for this, the child needs to understand why. For instance, David was angry because his half-sister Lisa lived with his mother and he did not. There had been an unsuccessful attempt to settle him back with his mother, but the changes in his family meant that they could not assimilate an older child.

My own map

This is a device we use to provide the child with a sense of movement through time. A child's conceptualisation is different to that of an adult; they have to think themselves back in time so such events as the most recent birthday, holiday, religious festivals, etc, are useful markers. Along with the child we map the moves of the birth family and the child's own moves since leaving them. Often we start with the geographical area where the birth mother was born and lived. This map may help a child to understand part of his or her own predicament if, for example, the birth mother had an unstable childhood with many moves too.

When working together on a map, it is important to remember that a child who has lived apart from his or her family of origin will have a different concept of time to your own. We have found that a child can conceptualise the length of the last school holiday and you can build on this. However, if you say, 'You lived for two years with your mother in this town,' it is likely to mean very little.

My life graph

We are grateful to the father of one of our families who developed the idea of a life graph. It is a simple diagram that helps the child, the worker and the new parents to understand the movements in the child's life. When we started using the life graph, we found resistance from children to working in what we saw as a logical order – from birth to the present day. To the children this was not logical. For them it was simpler to work back through time, starting from the present, echoing Joy Rees' approach – moving from the present to the past and then to the future.

Again, you can write the entries in pencil for the child to ink over or use erasable pens. Using different pens for colour-coding the different types of care (with birth parents, with foster carers, etc) can clarify the graph.

For pre-school children it may be necessary to introduce sensory stimuli such as smell, touch, sound and taste as well as visual stimuli and memories. For example, the child's life could be depicted as a train journey; this age group is usually familiar with Thomas the Tank Engine stories. The stations on the journey become significant stages in the child's life.

On the way through the life graph there will be painful events that children will want to avoid talking about in the early stages, but will eventually mention or allude to when they are feeling stronger and more secure. You can prepare a life graph in pencil and introduce it when talking about the child's birth, suggesting that they ink over that first entry. In the next

12th March – born in Maternity Hospital 6pm
I lived with Mary, my born to Mother and
Grandmother Croft. We lived at 117 Oak Street

My First birthday party
5th June. Grandmother Croft died

3rd November. High Meadow Nursery

My Second birthday
5th May. With Mary at 117 Oak Street

28th December. Leake Street Children's Home
3rd March. Lisa Lumb born
My third birthday
3rd June. With Mary and Paul Lumb
– Eastwood Road
20th November. The Children's Hospital
5th January. The Hollies Children's home
My fourth birthday

24th December. Peter and Joan Batt, foster Parents
My fifth birthday

9th August. Mary marries Dennis Lynch

22nd February. Anne Lynch born
My sixth birthday

29th May. Mary and Dennis Lynch, Duncan Terrace

5th January. Moved with family to Newton Gate
2nd February. The Haven Children's home
30th May. Eastfield Assessment Centre

12th November with Chris and Eddie

2002
2003
2004
2005
2006
2007
2008
2009
2010
2011

session, the child inks in the last entry, which is the present day. From there, you can ask them to ink in any section they wish and talk about this section together.

At first, most children will only be prepared to consider the less troubled periods of their lives, so do not expect any startling revelations. As the child inks over the "safe" periods, the uncompleted parts will indicate the periods about which they are unhappy and troubled. Younger children who cannot yet read or write can be encouraged to colour each segment of time. We find that this helps them to understand time and events. Birthdays are useful for marking the passage of time, especially if there are occasions about which the child may have happy memories.

The life graph is also valuable in predicting when possible setbacks may occur during the year – the anniversary effect. Claudia Jewett Jarrett, an American child and family therapist, believes that children can become unsettled for what appear to be unexplained reasons. She puts this down to the fact that some trauma may have occurred in the child's past and when the time in the year that it happened comes round again, this unsettling incident can cause problems in the present. Claudia Jewett Jarrett attributes this to the child's in-built clock being linked to the seasons of the year and the daylight hours that then trigger the response. It is often possible, therefore, to predict when unsettling events may occur.

ASLAM

Aslam had suffered two traumatic and distressing experiences in the month of March. These events were separated by a gap of five years but, following the second trauma, his carers noticed that around this period of the year, Aslam was reluctant to attend school and, in fact, developed an illness which was not feigned, having to stay off school for several days with a heavy cold. When this pattern emerged, it was possible to help Aslam understand that traumas from the past were entering into and distorting his present. His carers found it helpful to look at his life story book again and talk about these events. As Aslam grew older and gained more life experience it increased his ability to understand and place in context what had happened.

The life graph can be varied to suit the needs of the child. We know of foster carers who have prepared a life graph of the birth parents too, so that the child can understand what was happening to them as well.

There are other ways of making a life graph: for example, as mentioned earlier, with young children we might draw a railway line with each station being a stage in their lives. This opens other possibilities – each station could contain information about and photographs of significant events. With pre-school and early school-age children, we sometimes make a life graph about Janet the squirrel that mirrors the moves and changes that the child has experienced in his or her own life and this can often facilitate talking about feelings. For instance, when Janet left her tree house to go and live in another part of the wood with a different squirrel family could lead to asking 'I wonder how she felt about this?'

Revisiting the past

Many children deny that events in their past have happened. The uncompleted sections on the life graph may indicate to you where their problems lie. If you are satisfied that children like this are familiar with many aspects of the life graph, we believe that taking them on a journey to visit all the places they have lived in can help to overcome this difficulty.

Such visits will entail careful preparation, not only of the child, but also of the people from the past, and must be carefully timed. It should never be a substitute for the actual life story work but should complement it. If we can accomplish the visits in one day, we do so. The preparations will

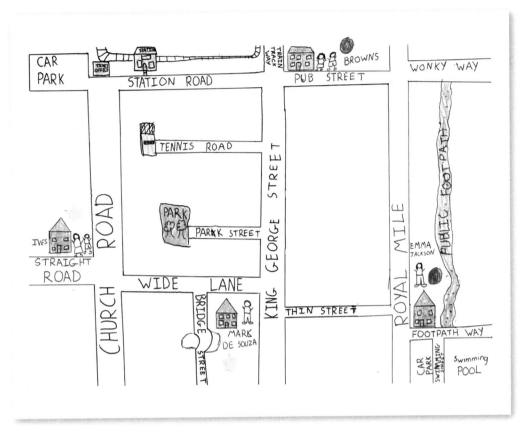

take longer and the work involved invariably means that the journey will have to be arranged by the child's social worker, who may need to make preliminary visits in order to prepare and explain the purpose of the visit.

The child's safety must also be considered in planning visits to places from their past, especially in cases of suspected but as yet undisclosed sexual abuse. Workers and carers need to be sensitive to the possibility of such visits reawakening repressed memories for traumatised children. The visits may also prompt some children to disclose experiences they had not talked about previously.

Whenever possible on these trips, work backward from the present using the child's life graph and personal map. This physical and geographical tracing of the child's life assists and enables them to place their life in context. It is invaluable in assisting you too, and it is inevitably a moving experience for all concerned. An unexpected bonus for us has been the warmth, affection and welcome received at each stopping place. Often children may have left these places abruptly, believing they have harmed and damaged people. To discover that they have not can be a relief and, therefore, an additional dividend.

At a later stage when "bridging" children into the future and using the candle technique (see Chapter 8), we are able to refer back to this journey and to the positive benefits to the children of having people in their past who loved them.

These trips can also be used to take photographs of significant people and places, and to simulate earlier events, which are then captioned in the life story book or stored in files or on film.

SHAUN

How these visits help children to begin to acknowledge their past and to face up to painful events in their lives showed clearly with Shaun. He had denied any knowledge of the time he spent at Downs Nursery even when he was taken there. For him to admit he had lived there was to acknowledge that his mother had been unable to care for him adequately. The cook and matron remembered him with affection and told tales of his early childhood – normally the function of parents. Afterwards, Shaun walked upstairs and into a bedroom, and said: 'That was my bed and I used to watch the trains from that window.'

Photographs about me

Photographs are an invaluable and essential part of life story work. They are not only a record of past events but also a means by which a child may be able to talk about the past and express feelings about it. However, you must avoid the trap of turning life story work into simply producing a photograph album with captions. The photographs are there to provide you with a focus for working together. We suggest that you may, alongside making a book or video, help the child to make a separate album of photographs. A photograph can be stuck on to a blank sheet of paper and used alongside the life graph and family tree. The child can write captions to the photo that link their knowledge of all three components. Although children will be interested in the photographs, they may be reluctant to use the sensitive ones in a life story book.

DAVID

David asked to keep the photograph of his birth mother and was allowed to do so, but we retained copies too as we were uncertain about whether or not he would destroy the others because they evoked such painful memories. Of course, the back-up computer file is invaluable.

David dictated under a photograph taken at Christmas:

I spent Christmas with my mum, Lisa, Anne and Dennis at New Town Estate. Lisa and Anne got bikes and I got a toy car. It's not fair, Lisa and Anne live with my mum and I don't. Dennis is OK; he used to give me rides on his motorbike. My mum used to shout and hit me with a belt. It's not fair Mr Hughes and the staff at Eastfield keep me from going home to my mum. I hate them. When I was with my mum I jumped on the settee and made a hole in it.

David dictated at another session:

This is me on a donkey at Filey. I went with my mum, Lisa, Uncle James and Paul Lumb for the day. My mum was not a bad person. She was not good at looking after little ones.

The photographs of his mother had a deep emotional impact, but he eventually placed them in his life story book and dictated:

Mary wants me to be adopted but I want Mary to adopt me.

At the following session he dictated:

This is my first mum Mary and my dog. She gave the dog away. It made me sad because she gave the dog away. It makes me sad because I cannot live without her.

David's captions show how photographs can help a child to talk about and express feelings. Certain photographs will be more significant because of the importance the child attaches to them. For example, we spent two sessions on the three photographs of David's mother, whereas seven pictures of his foster carers were dealt with in half a session. The reason for this was that the photographs of David's mother provided a means of discussing his relationship with her, the hurt he felt at not living with her, and a shift towards a realisation that to return to her was not possible. It was a start at helping him to understand that his mother cared about him even though her circumstances meant she could not care for him.

David was obviously pleased with all his photographs and wanted to show them and share them with his friends. This raised another problem. His life story book contained information that was personal and confidential, not for general consumption. How could he share the photographs but not the information? We asked ourselves how our own children did this: the answer was by using the family album. David was provided with a separate album to share.

Films about me

Easy to use smartphones, camcorders and digital cameras make possible the inclusion of film recordings, DVDs, memory cards and clips in life story work, either to be included in a book, or as the complete story, or for use in the work to help children come to terms with their past. The impact of a recorded interview with a parent, relative or family friend will be great. If a parent wants to give an explanation as to why they could not cope at the time the child separated from them, but could not face talking to the child direct, they can do so on film.

Similarly, if previous neighbours want to describe the birth family or remember their experiences of the child, they can do so on film for the child to keep. A film of a previous house, or foster family, or residential unit will be more immediate than photographs. Cine film can be reformatted to digital formats so that old holiday films or films of babies and children can be kept by the child. More and more film recordings are being kept by families and can be copied for the child to keep. A creative teenager, with appropriate preparations, can even go off to make their own film recordings with their telephone or a camera (yes, they usually bring the camera back!) of past places and people. The use of films can considerably enhance life story work in all sorts of ways and will be worth considering whenever this work is undertaken (see Chapter 14 for an introduction to using digital media, and *Digital Life Story Work* (Hammond and Cooper, 2013) for a full exploration of how to use these techniques).

This case study shows how a life story book and visits and photographs worked for one child.

JASON

Jason was 13 years old when he was placed with Claudia, a single woman in her late 40s, and Verna, her widowed mother. It was his ninth placement and he came direct to them from his third foster placement breakdown. Jason's parents had separated before he was born. His mother, who already had one child, was estranged from the extended family and without help or support. She left Jason in the hospital where he was born, believing he would be adopted. Jason was placed with elderly foster carers and stayed with them for eight years until he was removed because he was refusing to go to school. What follows is an account of how we untangled and came to understand Jason's past through a life story book.

Jason wrote in his life story book:

> *My first foster mother, who I thought was my real mum, used to spoil me. She let me do anything. We used to tie sheets together and play at Tarzan. The social worker took me on holiday because I asked him if he would. He took me to a residential unit. I was upset when I found out I was not going back to my foster mother.*

It was very difficult to make Jason's life story book because we had photographs only from his first foster home and one photograph taken in a residential unit when he was ten years old. Very little was known about his birth parents. There was only one thing to do: visit the area around the city where he had spent most of his life and experienced three foster homes and five residential units. This Claudia, Jason and I, as his social worker, did, starting with the maternity hospital where he was born.

Jason wrote afterwards:

> My mum asked me if I would like to go to my home town to see all my old friends and residential unit which I had stayed in. I am happy at home with my mum, grandma and the dogs. There are lots of things that have happened that I would rather like to forget, but I did want to show mum and grandma where I used to play, the shops, park and river.

Claudia wrote too:

> I was surprised that Jason could remember so much about the area, he seemed to know where every street and road came out – Jason had come to life, this was where he had enjoyed himself as a young lad. I could not help but feel happy for him as we strolled around hand in hand.

The day was exhausting, enjoyable and rewarding. Move after move, Jason was welcomed back with genuine affection at each place we visited. Claudia said afterwards that it laid to rest a lot of ghosts: it helped her to understand and become closer to Jason but it also made her feel angry at what had happened to her "son".

After this the next major step did not seem so big. I traced and visited Jasmine, his birth mother, who had last seen him as a baby. Taking my camera with me, I explained about Jason's life story book and she willingly allowed me to photograph her. In exchange, I gave her recent photographs of Jason. Jasmine was now remarried with two children, her oldest child living with her first husband. She also provided detailed information about her own family and I was able to give this to Jason for his life story book.

The next step was to arrange a meeting between Jason and Claudia with Jasmine and her second husband and family. This was done and, at the same time, Jasmine signed her consent for Claudia to adopt Jason. This meeting, which was fraught with potential risks, went smoothly from the moment Jason produced his life story book to show Jasmine. From there on, a meeting was arranged with Errol, Jason's birth father, and Claudia and Jason. Again, information was provided for Jason's family tree: he had been named after Errol's younger brother. Errol, too, signed the consent to the adoption application.

(It should be stressed that these meetings were only arranged after all the participants clearly understood the purpose. At no time was it to test out whether Jason could be reunited with his birth parents. It was for Jason's sake to dispel any secret dreams and fears he might have had about them and to free him emotionally from his past.)

Fifteen months after Jason went to live with Claudia, she adopted him. Two months after this, Claudia allowed him to spend a week with Jasmine and her family. (Claudia enjoyed not having to ask a social worker for permission.) The following week Claudia and Verna collected Jason and his half-brother and sister and took them to spend a week with Errol, who now lives with his parents and his elder son.

For the first time in his life, Jason is enjoying school, self-assured, confident and secure in the knowledge that Claudia loves him. We rarely talk about the past now: there is too much happening in the present and much to look forward to in the future.

8 Bridging: past, present and future

We use the term "bridging" for the time when we link the past and the present and provide a bridge to the future. We have slowly come to the conclusion that successfully "bridging" children is a crucial factor in them remaining in their permanent substitute family.

In doing the life story work together, you will have gained unique insight into and information about the child's past. This will prove invaluable in preparing the new family before the child arrives. Moving to a new family or returning to a birth family is a stressful time for children and they need help and support to cross the "bridge". It is a time when past, present and future can be placed in context and ghosts and fantasies laid to rest.

Vera Fahlberg suggests, and we too have found, that a child about to move into a new family is in a state of aroused anxiety. But it is often possible to deal with earlier unresolved attachment and separation issues by talking about a child's life experiences through life story work.

Kay Donley considers that appropriate bridging messages should be incorporated throughout life story work. She has identified the task, at this stage and in the early stages of placement, as one of disengaging the child from significant parental figures in the past, usually the birth mother, and assisting the child to engage with the "new" mother. Vera Fahlberg describes the process as one of obtaining "emotional permission" in order that the child can attach him or herself to the new family. Within the child's experiences there will be a hierarchy of people, starting with the birth mother, who can signal the message of disengagement and start the process of emotional permission to move towards a new family. At this important stage, it is essential to re-read a child's life story book to make sure that you have not overlooked clues about hidden anxieties and worries.

DAVID

With David, it became evident that the various statements he had written about his mother indicated a strong attachment to her, which was a mixture of reality and fantasy. His life story book contained several questionnaires and within these David had specifically mentioned his mother. For example:

David's birth mother had provided information and photographs of

The person I most like – my mother

My face has a big smile when – I see my mother

Things I worry about – my mother

I would not like to live without – my mother

his early life. She had been involved in the plans to place him with an adoptive family and had stated she would consent to his adoption. Through her involvement in helping with material for David's life story book, the concepts of disengagement and emotional permission were explained to her. When David had lived with his new family for nine months, a farewell meeting was arranged. At this meeting his mother signalled her approval of David's new parents. David was aware that his mother had consented to his adoption and given her "permission" for him to attach himself to his new family.

It is not always possible to involve birth parents in this way, either because they cannot be found or because they are contesting the adoption plan for their child and feel unable to be involved; nonetheless, it may be possible to get them to participate at a later stage. Kay Donley suggests that you go to the next person in the child's hierarchy. This might be either a previous foster carer or another adult with whom the child has made a significant relationship, such as a member of staff in a residential unit. She believes that a child's social worker does not have this significance. A successful way is to have a life appreciation day as we describe elsewhere. Details of previous carers will be contained in the child's file.

Saying "hello" and "goodbye"

We were inspired when we heard Claudia Jewett Jarrett talk about the importance of saying "hello" and "goodbye". We suggest that work is to be done in conjunction with the use of the life graphs described earlier.

Typically, a child, before being looked after, may have had several moves already and will possibly experience several moves between, for example, residential units and/or foster carers. Many of these moves will have been made in a crisis, unplanned and regrettably unexplained. This may have been the case while the child was living with his or her own family, and almost certainly when the child started to be looked after away from the family, and the chance to say "goodbye" properly was lost.

In a child's memory, the moves become a blur and events merge into each other. This can be damaging and add to the child's lack of confidence and impair a child's sense of identity. If you are working with a child in preparing for a move from, for example, a temporary foster home to an adoptive family, it presents a golden opportunity to rework some of the earlier experiences that might have been traumatic.

We describe below the well-established candles ritual and nowadays we can enhance this by introducing other "hello" and "goodbye" rituals. For example, if a child is leaving a temporary foster carer to move to a permanent new family, we encourage the foster carer to hold a farewell party. Similarly, if the child is moving school, due to changing families, we encourage the school to ritualise this by formally recognising the child's departure. These ritualised endings are especially important if the child has made significant attachments during a stay with a family or in a residential unit.

An "Advent" or "Moving" Calendar

Once children learn that a decision has been made for them either to return to their birth family or be introduced to a new family, their anxiety level rises. One reason for this is that children feel that these plans are outside their control. The process of moving therefore becomes frightening and confusing. We have found that making what we call an "Advent" or "Moving" calendar can reduce the uncertainty that may surround the move.

An Advent calendar has doors and windows that open to reveal aspects of the Christmas season during the countdown period to Christmas Day. In the same way the doors in a Moving calendar open up during the countdown to a placement. Usually visits home or to a new family are planned over several weeks during the period of introductions. The doors in the Moving calendar display a date. When they open they reveal a certain amount of specific information. The illustration shows an example of what such a calendar might reveal.

The candles ritual

The candles ritual is a way, at the "bridging" stage, of demonstrating to children that they have the capacity to love people. Children enjoy rituals and they can be used to help understand a particular idea. We borrowed the candle technique from Claudia Jewett Jarrett, who describes it in her book, *Adopting the Older Child*. We have used it on many occasions with children as young as two years to 14-year-olds; it demonstrates to the child that not only have they got the capacity to love, but that it is also safe to love others.

A row of candles is used to represent all the people the child has loved in his or her life. In front of this row, you place a candle to symbolise the child. While lighting this candle, you explain that it represents the child's birth, when he or she came into the world with an inborn ability to love people. Next, if it is significant, you light the first candle representing the birth mother and explain that this was the first person the child loved. You continue the process down the line, lighting a candle for each new situation the child moved into and each new person who was loved. Tell the child that because they were born with the ability to love people, it is not necessary to put out (extinguish) the love of the previous carer before loving another.

This technique illustrates how important it is to keep love alive. Usually we only use it when a new family is imminent, for it reveals that it is safe for the child to light the candles representing the new family. Once the child is with the new family, we repeat the ritual with the new parents to emphasise how important it is not to extinguish the love the child has for others from the past.

ELLIE

Perhaps Ellie best summed up the experience when she said, 'The candles I have just lit for John and Sally [her new parents] are burning the brightest and Lorraine's [her birth mother] candle, lit first, is burning down and will gradually fade away.'

Six months later, Ellie's relationship with her new mother was showing signs of strain. She was able to discuss this with Ellie by reminding her of the candle ritual, commenting that perhaps she felt she had been let down by mother figures in the past and now she was afraid to light a candle for her. Ellie was eventually able to recognise this and accept her assurance that it was safe to light her candle.

The ecomap

Vera Fahlberg, in *A Child's Journey Through Placement* (1994), describes what is called an "ecomap", originally developed as an initial interviewing tool to open communication between the child and social worker (Vera Fahlberg acknowledges the work of Marietta Spencer of the Residential Unit Society of Minnesota for this idea). It shows the child and the various people, places and concerns that form a part of his or her life. Children can discuss these elements and how they relate to them and so gain further understanding of their life as a whole and why they are where they are.

We have successfully taken this idea and adapted it for use not only during the bridging period but also when the child is in the new home. Then it becomes a means of helping the child and the new family to understand in pictorial form what we believe is happening. Vera Fahlberg considers it works best with children between five and twelve years old but we have used it as effectively with older children.

A child's responses to the question: Why am I here? will help you to perceive his or her understanding of their situation. You can then refer to the life story work you have done together to discuss the significant people in the child's life and illustrate their present relationship and the type of contact they have. For example:

My birth mum – writes me letters and speaks to me on the telephone.

My social worker – telephones me and visits me.

DAVID

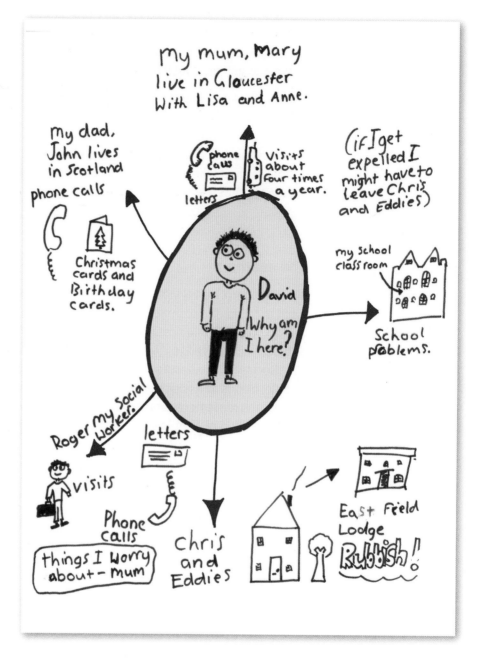

After David had been living with his new family for three months, he began to have behavioural problems at school that led to him being threatened with exclusion. We used David's ecomap to arrive at an understanding of how his behaviour at school was threatening his future with his new family. On the line from his new home to school he drew arrows attacking it, but shortly after this, his extreme behaviour subsided and, whilst his difficulties remained for a time, the threat of exclusion was removed.

Aspects of parenting

We always use Vera Fahlberg's "three parents" as a means of helping children during the bridging period. It has many uses, for example, demonstrating to children that it is not possible to take away from them what was given to them at birth by their parents. Below is an extract from her book, *A Child's Journey Through Placement* (1994). (Note that she uses the term "foster care" in the American sense, to include both foster care and residential care.)

> *Many children are given little information when they are moved. The foster care system may seem familiar and logical to social workers and foster carers but it frequently makes no sense to children. They need to know that foster families are families that take care of children when their birth parents cannot.*

LEGAL PARENT
Financial responsibility
Safety and security
Where you live
Where you go to school
Sign for operations
Permission to travel abroad
Sign for marriage under age
Sign for going into services
under age

BIRTH PARENT
Life itself
Gender
Ethnicity
Physical looks
Religion
Intellectual potential
Predisposition for certain
diseases
Basic personality type
(such as shy, stubborn,
active)

PARENTING PARENT
Love
Provides food, toys, clothes
Gives hugs and kisses
Disciplines
Takes care of you when sick

Recent legislation in the UK, and most recently the Adoption and Children Act 2002 (England and Wales), with its emphasis on parental responsibility, and the possibility of shared parental responsibility, has had a bearing on the concept of Vera Fahlberg's "three parents", especially the "legal parent". Nonetheless, despite the changes, we have retained the original concept in this edition because we regard it as a useful method not only of helping children to understand what has happened to them but, with the increased involvement of birth parents, it serves to help them to understand the legal and emotional aspects too. We have now modified the "three parents" – see opposite.

PARENT WITH LEGAL RESPONSIBILITY
Financial responsibility
Safety and security
Where you live
Where you go to school
Sign for operations
Permission to travel abroad
Sign for marriage under age
Sign for going into services under age

BIRTH PARENT
Life itself
Gender
Ethnicity
Physical looks
Religion
Intellectual potential
Predisposition for certain diseases
Basic personality type (such as shy, stubborn, active)

"LOOKING AFTER" CARER
Love
Provides food, toys, clothes
Gives hugs and kisses
Disciplines
Takes care of you when sick

The three parents — modified

Despite the legislative changes, the emotional aspects remain unchanged for the child, especially the strong feelings about his or her birth parents and the confusion of being parted from them. The terminology and/or precise application of the underlying concept may need to be altered to meet the precise circumstances of the child (e.g. whether he or she is in care or accommodated) and whether or not the placement is with adoptive parents, special guardians or in kinship care. What is important is that the child – and the child's birth parents – have a right to an understandable explanation of how they fit into the legal framework, but there is a corresponding right to understand that their birth endowment remains unchanged for life and that no-one can either alter this or take it away; it is a fact of their very existence.

Vera Fahlberg (1994) continues:

Everyone has birth parents, a birth mother and a birth father. These will be the same two people for all of a person's lifetime. No one can change this. Children in our society also have legal parents. Legal parents make the major decisions in a child's life. "Parenting parents" meet the child's daily needs for nurture and discipline.

For many children, birth parents are also the legal parents and the parenting parents. However, in foster care and adoption the different aspects of parenting are split. The child in foster care still has the same set of birth parents as he/she had prior to placement. In some cases where an agency has obtained a court order, the legal parenting role is shared by the birth parent and the agency or court. In the case of foster care being arranged at the request of the birth parent, that birth parent will continue to be the legal parent.

When a child is returned to the birth home, but the agency continues to supervise the placement, Figure 3 (see figure on previous page). can be used to help explain different people's responsibilities. The birth parent has again become the parenting parent but some aspects of the legal parent role related to safety and security may be retained by the agency or court.

A court order may be made transferring to the agency, using the social services/social work department, many of the responsibilities of the legal parent. However, the child continues to have the same birth parents although these adults no longer have the same legal rights or responsibilities. The foster carers continue to be the parenting parents. In explaining adoption to a child, he/she can be told that no one set of parents will again fill all three parenting roles. However, adoption is the combining of two aspects of the parenting roles – the legal parent and the parenting parent. Adoption means that the parenting parents now have all of the legal rights and responsibilities but they are not the birth parents. This fits as well for infant adoption as for older child adoption. After a child is adopted, the parents with whom the child lives, rather than social workers or the legal system, will be in charge of the major decisions in the child's life.

Life story work as a reference point

Life does not run smoothly, so you can expect even a well-prepared child to present problems in the new setting. Most of these will be normal behaviour, but occasionally inappropriate behaviour may have its origins in earlier life experiences, for example, David's fear of loving Chris, his adoptive mother. Vera Fahlberg likens the process to that of a telephone switchboard where the child's past becomes plugged into their present and begins to interfere with and distort it. Life story work may help to identify what has led to this problem and a life story book can be used, at a time of crisis, as a reference point.

Life story work and the way it is documented represents a point of view based on information that was available at the time the work was undertaken. It is important that neither you nor the child regards the work as static or complete simply because a book is produced. Life experiences and the normal developmental process mean that past experiences will be re-examined in light of new ones.

STACEY

Stacey, an 11-year-old girl, was having difficulties settling into her new family and her new parents were having difficulty adjusting to her too. It was possible to turn to her life story book, where similar incidents had occurred, and use it as a reference to point to the difficulties of living in a family. Stacey was struggling with assimilating herself into her new family. She had experienced two foster placement breakdowns and she was becoming anxious that her third placement was about to disrupt. It was by helping her express these fears and linking them to painful events in her past that she could begin to understand how her past was interfering with her present. Stacey then wrote the following:

I want to stay with Margery and John and for them to be my mum and dad. It is hard to build up a new family. When I fell out with my mum and dad I felt upset. He said if I don't change my attitude I will have to go. I want to change my attitude. When I quarrel with my mum it makes me feel miserable. It makes me worried because I might have to leave home. I would like to stay with Mum and Dad because it is the right place to be. There is nowhere else to go really. I want to co-operate with other people but it is hard to understand how to do this. I got on with my dad alright and I love them both. I won't go on being miserable and having no friends. I don't understand why I can't make friends because I had friends at Southgate Lodge.

We were able to show this to her new parents and the tension noticeably reduced. Her new parents were able to understand that Stacey's behaviour was not deliberate but was brought about by anxieties from her past that had leaked into her present.

9 Beyond life story work

For some children, life story work will not be sufficient to penetrate the barrier they have erected to protect their inner and painful world. We have found this particularly with children who have experienced numerous moves that have severely damaged their ability to form and sustain relationships beyond a superficial level. Such children used to be called "emotionally frozen", which Vera Fahlberg defines as having an over-investment in the past, into which all energies seem to go, creating an emotional imbalance. Nowadays, we recognise such a child as having attachment difficulties, and *The Attachment Handbook for Foster Care and Adoption* (Schofield and Beek, 2006) describes different types of attachment, attachment formation and lists useful "attachment tasks" for carers.

The trauma of separation from the birth parent is probably the worst any child will ever experience. Its effects should never be under-estimated or ignored, even if many years have passed. Children may become fixated or "emotionally frozen" as a result of this separation, and the risk of breakdown in a permanent family placement is very high because their shallowness seems to invite rejection. After several placements, such children begin to attract labels that describe them as immature, superficial in relationships, indiscriminate in affection, self-centred, and so on.

You will have noticed from David's life graph that he had nine moves in seven years, and was just such a child with attachment difficulties. Children like David hardly ever feel able to talk in an adult way about themselves. They need to find other ways of communicating and we need to find other ways of communication with them. There are lots of different methods, but essentially they are all based on the sort of communication that children themselves favour: using play as a means of communication and working through a situation. However, for some children, skilled therapeutic intervention will be necessary before life story work can begin.

Communication through play

What follows is not about therapy in the usually accepted sense, but suggests ways of communicating with children, which we have used successfully. Anyone who has seen children being parents to their dolls and copying their parents' ways of talking will realise that this is a good way for us to get through to children. To do this makes demands on us as adults, because it requires us to shed our inhibitions. We must enter the world of the child whilst being sensitive to what the child might be saying and being ready to respond accordingly.

We have used these play techniques with children aged from three to 15 years old. As we have gained confidence in using them, we have introduced these techniques into our preparation of life story work rather than at the end, and now we often use play before we start life story work.

Glove puppets

Having one glove puppet to speak for you and another for the child to speak through is a useful way to talk with children of all ages, but is particularly useful with younger children. No matter how good a relationship you have with a child, most find difficulty in revealing their inner world. They feel safer disclosing their intimate thoughts through puppets because of the distance the puppet seems to provide. Usually a two-way conversation can be started by your puppet asking the child's puppet questions. It is useful, wherever possible, not to ask direct questions but to speak via the puppets in the third person.

ASHA

The following is a conversation between a foster carer and Asha, a five-year-old girl who had recently experienced separation from her parents. They spoke to each other through Frog, a glove puppet (the foster carer) and a penguin puppet (Asha).

Frog *Do you live with Auntie Neeta and Uncle Anish?*

Penguin *Sometimes.*

Frog *I wonder where you would like to live?*

Penguin *With my mummy and daddy.*

Frog *Oh, if I could not live with my mummy and daddy I would feel very sad.*

Penguin *I feel sad because I cannot live with them.*

Frog *I wonder why you can't you live with your mummy and daddy?*

Penguin *Because they are no longer friends and do not love each other.*

Shortly after this conversation, Asha, who had not cried since the separation two weeks before, started to cry because "permission" to grieve had been given.

Play people

This technique can be used with young children aged three upwards with outstanding success, but can also be used with older children once you have overcome your own inhibitions. You need to be able to relax to join in this activity!

You can buy a "family" of play people at a toy shop. The set we use has been made with recognisable expressions, such as happiness, sadness, anger and so on. You can get play people of different ethnic backgrounds. These can be used to represent police officers, judges and other people who played a significant part in the child's story.

Children who are reluctant to talk directly about how they feel are prepared to talk about how the play people "feel". The technique involves telling a story that is basically the child's life story as depicted in the life graph, but transferred to the play people. Telling the story for the first time, we usually just talk about concrete facts: 'This is the mummy and she had a baby girl.' Eventually the child is drawn into the play – which may carry through several sessions – and will start to attribute feelings to the play people which mirror his or her inner world.

Children who have been subjected to acts of violence will frequently work out these experiences again. One child hurled the father figure around the room. Another five-year-old, Chloe, was confused because her elderly short-term foster carer had cried when she was moved to an adoptive family. Six months later she was still puzzled, but refused to talk about the incident. With the play people we were able to tell her a story about the little girl who had to move from her "Nan" whom she loved and this "Nan" cried. Chloe said, 'When I moved from my Nan she cried and I wanted to cry too but I was afraid to.' From this she was helped to understand what had happened and given reassurance that her "Nan" was safe and well.

The empty chair

Children will accumulate resentment against adults from their past who have either disappointed or rejected them. Occasionally these feelings can be detected, but usually they remain guarded and unresolved. One way to reach out and bring them into the open is by using the "empty chair" technique, a Gestalt therapy technique that we found in Claudia Jewett Jarrett's *Adopting the Older Child*.

Place an empty chair in the centre of the room. Ask the child to imagine that a person with whom he or she has some unfinished business is seated on it. The empty chair helps the child to focus on anything that is left unfinished.

David was interested and curious when we presented him with the empty chair. But he claimed he was unable to think of a suitable occupant for it. 'How about your mother?' we prompted. David then walked purposefully up to the chair and demanded to know, 'Why did you leave me? I want to kick your head in.' With a nervous laugh, he half-heartedly attempted to retract the statement. 'I wonder if you are angry with your mother?' we asked. 'Yes I am,' he replied.

It is often possible to use such expressions of anger constructively by encouraging the child to take over the role of the person in the chair so as to experience how the other person feels.

David sat in the chair and imagined he was his mother, while I pretended to be David. 'Why did you leave me?' I asked. 'I left you because I was quarrelling with your dad and we couldn't live together any more,' came his reply.

The telephone

A telephone can be used in a similar way to an empty chair. Your child can be encouraged to "telephone" a person from the past and have an imaginary conversation with that person. Frequently this is too direct, but can be made less threatening by holding a telephone conversation between puppets or dolls.

CHANTELLE

Chantelle had been removed from her birth family as a four-year-old because she had suffered persistent cruelty from her mother's partner. She had been placed in a foster family, but this had broken down after six months. Four months after this breakdown, the following play with dolls and a telephone took place. We made two sets of parents with dolls; the father in one set had an angry face. The dolls were not given names and were not identified as foster carers or birth parents.*

* This study first appeared in an article in Community Care in December 1982.

Me *Look at this little girl* [doll]. *She cannot live with her birth mummy. Do you think she will ever take love and care from this forever mummy and daddy?*

Chantelle *No, she can only take love and care from her birth mummy and that man who lives with her is good.*

Me (Gently) *I do not think he is.*

Chantelle *Well, he is.* (Chantelle then picked up the angry male doll and moved him away from the mummy doll.)

Me *Look what happens.* (I took the mummy doll to the angry male doll and reunited them.)

Chantelle *But he had gone away.* (She picked up the angry male doll and threw it across the room.)

Me *Now look what happens. The birth mummy goes and gets him back.*

We enacted this several times with Chantelle hurling the angry male doll away and me taking the mummy doll to collect it. Chantelle was getting exasperated and announced she was going to 'telephone that mummy'. She was already familiar with the telephone because we had played with it in the past.

Me *What do they call the mummy?*

Chantelle *Carmen* (the name of her birth mother) *Hello! I want to know why that little girl cannot live with you. Why don't you get rid of the man so this little girl can come and get love and care?*

(At this point Chantelle held the telephone out, a look of consternation and disbelief on her face.)

Me *What is the matter?*

Chantelle *She put the phone down on me.*

A powerful urge to pick Chantelle up and comfort her hurt almost overwhelmed me. With some effort of will, I concentrated on the doll play.

Me *Poor little girl, she is in such a whirl. (I spun the little girl doll around.) She doesn't know where to go. She can't get love from her birth mummy and will not take love from the forever mummy and daddy.*

Chantelle *Yes, she is all empty inside.*

Chantelle decided to telephone the little girl and advise her to go and live with the forever mummy and daddy because she could get love and care from them. I suggested to Chantelle that we should tell her we understand why she wants to love her birth mummy too.

Chantelle *Yes, I know. She can love her birth mummy, but she cannot live with her because her mummy does not want this man to go.*

Shortly after this Chantelle moved in and eventually settled with a new family.

At no time was this play interpreted to Chantelle. For instance, obviously we felt she was the little girl doll, but we never attempted to make this link for her. Violet Oaklander, in *Windows to our Children*, considers that the process of work with the child is a gentle, flowing one, 'an organic event'. The work for Chantelle using the dolls and telephone helped her to understand events in her life and start the process of coming to terms with them in a way that was non-threatening. We feel that if we had faced her with direct questions about why her foster placement disrupted, nothing would have been forthcoming.

Role play

With older children, particularly adolescents, one can be more direct. We frequently role-play situations by suggesting to the teenagers that we will be them and that they be another actor in the scene. This means that they have to "direct" and be the "scriptwriter" too. This can be a revealing experience for all concerned.

We discuss role-play further in the section about working with adolescents in groups in Chapter 11.

10 Working with black and minority ethnic children

When talking to children about their family history, background and future, you will come across many misconceptions they have about themselves and you will find many opportunities to give them more information about themselves, thereby helping them to have a more positive self-image. For Asian, African and African-Caribbean children and children of mixed heritage, there is an extra dimension to their feelings about themselves – their skin colour and what this signifies. Preparation for life story work always needs to be handled with extreme care and honesty, especially when you are trying to put things into their true perspective, and possibly even more so when you are working with black children and children of mixed heritage – particularly if you are white.

At the start, if you are white and are doing life story work with such a child, you should be familiar with the correct terminology to use when referring to black and minority ethnic people, as incorrect usage of words may inhibit rather than help. Terms such as "coloured" are offensive and should never be used. They deny the child's ethnic identity.

If you are white, you should recognise that, for the child, talking to a white person about "race" and racism is a poor substitute for talking to a black/minority ethnic person. You should therefore make every effort to involve a black/minority ethnic worker. Through this helper, many questions can be answered at first hand and a link will be provided with a person with whom the child may be able to identify. This can be particularly useful for children who have been looked after for a great part of their lives and may have had little contact with people from their own ethnic community, or for children who are living far removed from their culture or who have been placed transracially or transculturally from overseas.

In many areas of the UK, black and minority ethnic children who are separated from their birth families are in a tiny minority and white people are the dominant group. For self-protection, or because they have few other models, these children may identify with being "white" and tolerate racist remarks. Black and minority ethnic children who "think" they are white or try to make themselves white (by scrubbing their skins, for example) are set for a very destructive phase in the future. As with all our children, we need to help them build a positive self-image and to give them a good sense of self-esteem. We need to help them to realise that it is not their being black or Asian or of mixed heritage that is the problem, but other people's attitudes to it. However, we also need to keep this matter in perspective and recognise that it is only one of the areas of potential difficulty for them, and that other areas in their lives and identity also need to be given importance.

A book titled *Working with Black Children and Adolescents in Need*, edited by Ravinder Barn (1999), is a collection of articles that focus on communicating with black and minority ethnic children, and which also discuss various aspects and techniques of doing direct work with them.

White workers should carefully consider and work through their own fears and doubts and not underplay issues of "race", racism and colour. Otherwise, any discomfort or inhibition will communicate itself to the child who will instinctively sense these barriers. This can lead to communication becoming strained and the child feeling unsafe and unable to trust the worker.

What can you do?

Issues about "race", racism and ethnic identity are highly complex and charged with feelings, so much so that workers – both black/minority ethnic and white – may need a consultant to talk through issues of ethnicity and culture, to help put their feelings in perspective. This can help free the workers to clearly define areas that are problematic for them as distinct from those that are problematic for the child.

It is important to a child that the worker doing life story work has a good grasp of the child's world, both the inner world and external realities. This means the worker must familiarise him or herself with aspects of family life of the ethnic community of the child in the context of this society. This involves getting information from a variety of sources, for example, people from a culture similar to that of the child, and of course the internet.

Black and minority ethnic people are generally perceived as a homogeneous group and this leads to the vast differences in patterns of family life and child rearing being overlooked by professionals. There are enormous cultural, ethnic and class differences in family lifestyles among people around the world and reflected in the minority ethnic communities in UK society. These differences need to be understood and their importance acknowledged.

A child needs to feel valued by the worker and this feeling transmits itself to the child who very soon will get a sense of an adult who knows 'what it feels like when there aren't any words to say it'. Learning about the child's world demonstrates in a concrete way the value the worker puts on the child.

It is important to remember that a child's life story does not stop with the move to the new family. In birth families, children are regularly reminded of characteristics they have inherited from relatives and given news of family members and other important people in their lives. This continuity should also be provided for children growing up in substitute families.

Whatever your ethnic background, if you are doing life story work with a black, minority ethnic or mixed heritage child, you need to recognise the ongoing need of that child to talk about their ethnicity when he or she wishes to. When talking about family life, give children pictures of families from different ethnic backgrounds. Ask them to talk about the people in the pictures and ask which most closely resemble them. Use this as a starting point for discussion. Ask the child to draw a picture of him or herself, as they would like to look. If they present a picture other than of how they are, use this for discussion of people of different ethnic backgrounds and their characteristics, stressing the uniqueness of the individual.

All children need a sense of their ethnic and cultural background as well as of their family background. Try to get hold of pictures, posters and books of the child's (or their family's) community of origin (see Further Reading for titles of some useful books). (Do the same for white children from other countries.) Include pictures of famous black and minority ethnic people, especially British black and minority ethnic people – writers, politicians, musicians and sportsmen and women – in the collection of material. Stress the achievements of the child's community when the opportunity arises. There is much information online, so look this up so that you are prepared to share.

Visit or write to different community information centres and youth clubs to see what help they can give you. Children may want to know about subjects such as Islam or Rastafarianism, about what kind of food their birth families would eat, what festivals they may celebrate, and about how they should look after their hair and skin. Help them to find out about all these things. If there are festivals in your area, such as a Caribbean carnival or an Asian mela, take the child to them. In Bristol, the Empire Museum with its exhibits from different countries, is another useful resource.

Life story work with children who are fostered or in residential care

DANIELLE

Danielle is of mixed heritage, with a father of African-Caribbean origin and a white British mother. Her mother had an unhappy home life and left home at an early age to go to Liverpool. There she met Danielle's father. They had a happy relationship and their first baby, Danielle's

sister, was welcome and well cared for. The relationship began to break down and when she found she was pregnant again, Danielle's mother was unhappy. By the time Danielle was born, her father had all but disappeared and Danielle's birth was an unwelcome event.

By the time she was four Danielle was in care; her older sister stayed with their mother. An attempt was made to place Danielle in a long-term foster home, but this did not work out. Her mother was still concerned about her, but did not feel that Danielle could ever return to her. When Danielle was eight years old, it was decided that a second attempt should be made to foster her. This time a life story book was made before the placement. During the process of making the book, it became clear that Danielle did not really believe that she had a father or that she was of dual heritage.

Danielle had said that she did not want to leave the residential unit she was living in and she would go and hide if her social worker came to talk to her about fostering. She agreed, however, to make a life story book because she wanted to know more about herself. By drawing her family tree, talking about her birth certificate and discussing the "facts of life", Danielle came to accept that she had a father and that he had a name and could be talked about.

The next stage was to get Danielle to accept that her father was black and that she therefore had a place in the black community as well as the white one. I offered to show her photographs of St Lucia, where her father had come from. Danielle eventually accepted this offer and started to talk to the other children and staff about her father. She faced derision from the other children but she was so fascinated by discovering her "other half" that it did not deter her.

Being of mixed heritage had bothered Danielle for a long time, but she had never found an opportunity to talk about it. Now that she could talk about it with more confidence, she could easily identify where her father had come from and she could see from her birth certificate who both her parents were. Because of her concern for Danielle, her mother had willingly given photographs of her before she came into care, although she had no photograph of Danielle's father.

By the time the life story book was up to date and Danielle had also been given the opportunity to discuss the breakdown of her previous placement, she felt secure enough in her sense of identity to consider trying again. She was placed with a new family – with a Jamaican father and white Irish mother – and felt happy talking to them about her birth parents, and saw this was accepted by them when she showed them her life story book. She was adopted by this new family a year later.

Danielle needed knowledge about all her past, part of which was that she was of mixed heritage. It was an important part of all the things she needed to sort out.

For help with this section we are grateful to Beulah Mills, Janis Blackburn, and Rose Dagoo.

An anthology published by BAAF, titled *In Search of Belonging* (Harris, 2006), is a collection of writings by over 50 children, young people and adults who have been adopted transracially, including from overseas. This collection illuminates their feelings and thoughts about having been adopted, and the struggles that many of them have faced in coming to terms with both their adoption as well as their ethnic and cultural identities.

Life story work with children adopted from overseas

Increasing numbers of children who were born in other countries are being adopted in the UK, not only from countries where economic conditions or natural disaster separate large numbers of children from their families but also where families from war-torn countries have sent their children to this country "unaccompanied". This may raise particular issues in the future if contact is re-established with the birth family and the child has grown up with one set of attitudes towards parental responsibilities that are different from those of the family that sent them to the UK.

There are also many unaccompanied asylum-seeking children who are either placed in foster care or with family and friends carers. For such children, there are added complications about their asylum status (and whether they feel safe enough to talk about what happened to them) in addition to the emotional trauma they may have been through. Very careful thought and discussion should take place before starting work with them, including possible consultation with organisations such as the Refugee Council.

Many of the children adopted from abroad are now adolescents, a time when a healthy sense of identity becomes especially important. In doing life story work with these children, there are added considerations for both the children and the adoptive parents. Many of the "basics" that one might assume when working with children born and brought up in the UK may not apply.

Societies are naturally structured differently in other countries and concepts of family, parenthood, and parental obligation can be different to what you may be used to; you need to be aware of these and sensitive to them when helping a child to understand his or her origins. This is especially important when looking at reasons why birth parents might have given up their child for adoption.

It is equally important when the parents of the child may not be known at all. Civil unrest, extreme poverty and extended family breakdown can all have meant that a child's origins are unknown and cannot be part of his or her life story work – the trail may only start from when the adopters met the child for the first time.

However, it is essential to get as much information as possible about the child's country of origin and customs and language and for these to be part of the work. If individual information and material are not available, then pictures of children in the country of origin will need to be substituted and carefully captioned so that the child does not wrongly assume that he or she is in the photograph. The issues raised earlier in this chapter are equally relevant in work with children from other countries.

Many countries of origin are portrayed in the media in a derogatory way and those doing life story work with the child may need to come to terms with this as the child will need to feel positive about his or her native country and will pick up from you how you feel about their country. Most adoptive parents will not share the child's origins and will need to appreciate the effect this might have – the child will feel that you do not understand his or her feelings about growing up in the UK when their origins lie elsewhere.

Similarly, children in the neighbourhood and at school may want to know where the child comes from – you can help by making the child secure about his or her origins and able to acknowledge that he or she comes from a different country and encourage the child to be proud of this heritage, not embarrassed about it. If this is not possible, then a good "cover story" will help.

Using maps will help the children orientate themselves. Remember to show maps of the countries in between their country and the UK, or use a world map, as well as maps of the country of origin and the UK, so that the child can see how they came to the UK.

Information and pictures of the country of origin will be available online. Also, in todays's multicultural society, there is every likelihood that there is a community, especially in urban centres, that represents the child's origins.This would be invaluable in helping you both to understand the culture, customs and everyday life of the country your child has come from. There are reliable sources on the internet and also a number of excellent personal narratives written by unaccompanied asylum seeking children from different countries.

If you decide to and are able to visit the country of the child's origin, this will need careful preparation but would be invaluable in helping the child to develop a healthy sense of identity. Consider carefully the question of contact with the birth family – you will need to judge if the child is ready to handle it.

Some countries make such trips difficult because they close the door behind the child after adoption. Records may be unreliable or may not have been kept, or they may have been destroyed. Some countries may have allowed dual citizenship but this brings obligations, such as military service, which they may expect to be fulfilled.

Record the trip and take photographs of all the people and places important to the child's origins and the story, particularly the place they were born and the place where they first met the adopters.

Some people suggest that if you are making a life story book you should make two – one about the child's story and one about the child's country of origin. If you do this, consider whether it conveys to the child a feeling of separation from his or her roots; each child will be different.

Adopters

You may be an adoptive parent doing life story work with your child.

The reasons for adopting your child will need to be part of the work. As well as the usual issues about why you decided to adopt, you will also need to address the fact that you chose to adopt a child from overseas.

You may have done this because there are so few babies for adoption in the UK now, or you may have heard and read stories of abandoned children or you may have worked in the country of origin and became close to that child. You may have wanted to provide a child with disabilities a chance of a successful life and treatment, which they could not have had if you had not adopted them.

Be aware of the implications of "rescuing" a child from their birth country or of people from a rich country adopting children from a poor country. Your child will identify with his or her country and with its people and if they feel "bad" or ambivalent about the country it will not help their sense of self-esteem and self-worth. You will need to try and ensure that you have the competence or support that will be needed to minimise the child losing their ethnic, cultural and linguistic background.

Through life story work, you can help your child develop a healthy sense of identity and integrate their cultural and personal history into their whole personality.

A collection of writing and poetry by adopted children, *The Colours in Me* (Harris (ed), 2008), contains a number of pieces by children adopted from overseas, who describe their feelings about adoption.

Some famous adopted people

Bill Clinton, former President of the United States, was looked after by his grandparents when young and adopted by his stepfather, taking his surname.

Steve Jobs, co-founder of Apple and inventer of the iPad and iPod, was adopted at birth.

John Lennon, musician in The Beatles, was adopted by his aunt as his mother was unable to look after him.

Nelson Mandela, human rights activist and former President of South Africa, was adopted at the age of nine.

Hannah Pool, journalist and author who has written for *The Guardian* for over a decade, was adopted internationally from Ethiopia.

Jamie Foxx, actor, director, producer and singer-songwriter, was adopted by his grandmother.

50 Cent, hip-hop musician, was adopted by his grandparents.

Nicky Campbell, TV and radio presenter, was adopted just days after he was born.

11 Working with groups

Working with families

When there is more than one looked after child in a family, it is possible to do some of the work of making a life story book together, but it is important that each child has his or her own separate record of their life story work. We have found that working with a family in a group progresses faster than working in a one-to-one situation. The work will, of course, depend on the ages of the children in the family. With older children you might consider using a modified form of the group programme for adolescents, described later on in this chapter. Nonetheless. in most families children's recollections of events can be different and there is a need to guard against children being retraumatised.

Normally it will be the oldest child who will provide the link for the others from past to present. That child may be the family "historian", assisting you in helping the other members of the family to understand what has happened in their past and what is happening in the present. In doing so, the older child is able to extend their own knowledge and understanding too, and can begin to explain to their siblings how they understand things. This can be less threatening than explaining to someone outside the family.

In working with sibling groups, again it is important to bear in mind the issue of undisclosed sexual abuse. It may be that only one child in a sibling group has disclosed, but that group discussion prompts other siblings to disclose. It is also important to remember that older siblings are more likely to have been pressured into silence themselves and could deny that abuse has taken place when younger members of the family disclose that they have been abused. In such situations, it may be more useful to do individual sessions with each of the siblings before doing work as a family group. Some children/young people might need additional individual sessions irrespective of whether sexual abuse has occurred.

Kinship care

Increasingly social workers are seeing the value of keeping children in the extended family or with close family friends when birth families break down. This is usually (but not always) preceded by a Family Group Conference in which solutions are explored and various family members make commitments to the children concerned.

This is a situation where confusion for the children concerned can arise. It is easy to assume that because they have remained within the extended family they are fully aware of what is happening and who the various family members are. The children concerned need to know who is who in the family, what the interconnections are, who the step-relatives are and how their birth family came to break down. How does the child feel about the arrangements, and what does the future hold? Life story work can resolve a lot of these questions and give a child a way of asking questions and talk about their feelings about what is happening. For family and friends carers, the thought of life story work can be particularly daunting in terms of how to approach it and how this might conflict with their sense of loyalty to the birth parents.

With a sibling group, we might ask how the oldest child can explain to the other siblings why they became separated from their family of origin.

MARIE

Marie, 14 years old and the eldest of four children, felt that she had been the cause of why they had to leave their birth family (because of her "bad behaviour"). When she declared this, it was a revelation to her to find out that a younger brother and sister also felt that they were the cause for the separation. From there, they were helped to reach an understanding of their mother's mental illness. They understood that there were reasons why they were now living with a foster family and that there was no need to seek to blame anyone, or take the blame upon themselves, because the causes were beyond their control.

Working with adolescents in groups

We have shown how working with children from the same family can help in the process of life story work. Working with a group of children who are not related can also be successful.

Children over 12 who have been looked after for many years become unwilling to talk about their past, confused about the present and have little sense of hope for the future. We have found that providing a setting in which children share their pasts, their feelings about the present and their hopes for the future with others who have experienced similar difficulties can be a help and a comfort. A group preparation can be a way of reducing the sense of isolation many children feel and a means of freeing them to share similar feelings with others.

Children who are looked after often consider that their families are abnormal and it can be a revelation to them that their families are like many others. One group of five children discovered in their exploration that not only had none of them ever met their fathers, or had not done so for many years, but also that they all came from many-fathered families and all had half-brothers and sisters. No amount of assurance from an adult could, have helped these children to place their families in context as "normal" as much as talking and sharing with their peers had.

To help get over the natural reluctance to discuss the past, present and future, we have worked out a programme of meetings (eight core meetings and then a few follow-up meetings) that divide roughly into three stages. The first stage is to help the young people to develop an awareness of themselves, to begin to express their inner thoughts and feelings, and to look at the range of options open to a looked after child – of which fostering is but one. How making a life story book might help is introduced as a discussion topic about half-way through this stage and books are made individually during the second stage.

"Bridging" work, the third stage, which is done partially within the group, can start only when the possibility of return to the birth family or a move to a foster family is imminent. Sometimes we have enlisted the help of children who have made life story books and who have been successfully placed during this bridging stage. This greatly facilitates discussion about hopes and fears, as well as injecting an element of reality.

Forming and working with a group

The group should be carefully selected. It is a working group that can perhaps accommodate one disruptive member, but rarely more. All the children's foster carers or social workers or residential social workers must have agreed in advance that they do life story work with their child and understand what they will be taking on in doing this. Meetings can be arranged with those involved with the child to explain the broad outline of what you are doing and to discuss the problems of possible regression.

Usually we work with six children and two to three leaders. The initial group work runs for eight weekly sessions of about one-and-a-half hours and includes the sharing of a simple meal. Planning and recording takes a further two-hour meeting of the leaders each week. At the third session, the idea of a life story book is introduced.

The aim of such a group is to provide an atmosphere in which the children can talk freely about their doubts and fears. Of course the comments we have made earlier about confidentiality apply here too. Our major source of ideas about the content of such group sessions comes from Violet

Oaklander's *Windows to our Children* and we suggest that you read this book as part of your preparation. We describe here the content of the group sessions, which, as with other ideas in this book, you may need to adapt to your own needs.

Depending on the time of year, and the time available, we have found it valuable to arrange a trip out early in the life of the group and additional to the normal sessions. This, we find, helps to form a group identity.

A programme for group work

Session 1

Before this first meeting, each child will have been visited by one of the leaders and been given an explanation of what will be happening.

The session starts with a brief explanation of the aims and purposes of the group and an introduction of the group members. Then we start work with some "warm up" exercises in which everyone is involved. For example, we sit in a circle and throw a ball between us, first calling out our own name and then throwing a ball to a group member and calling out their name, until the ball has been passed to each person.

We use the game 'I went to market and bought some apples'. The next person repeats this and adds a word beginning with the next letter of the alphabet. They might say, 'I went to market and bought some apples and bananas'. The next person might say, 'I went to market and bought some apples, some bananas and some cauliflowers,' and so on through the alphabet.

We then move on to a "quick-think" session. For this we have a flip chart mounted on an easel. The children call out ideas related to the topic under consideration and these are written down on the flip chart. If any child is prepared to do the writing we let them do so. Two or three topics can be covered in a session. The first quick-think topic is 'Why are we here?' We use the contributions on the flip chart as a basis for discussion and soon we break for a simple meal, during which the discussion continues.

We then have a quick-think session to create "Feelings" cards like those discussed earlier. The purpose of this activity is to introduce the concept of words to describe emotions. Ask the children to call out words that describe feelings, like sad, happy, angry, and so on. Write these down on individual cards. Then the group, including the leaders, draw faces to match the feelings. Continue this game with individuals miming a feeling.

The final quick-think session is on: 'What is a family?' The ideas of what constitutes a family are then used in the discussion. Remember at this stage not to force the pace of the group or try and lead it where it does not want to go.

Finish the session with some group game, perhaps a repetition of 'I went to market'.

Session 2

Open the session with the group's very own game, 'I went to market'. The group has to try and recall the correct sequence from the previous week. Return to the work on "feelings" cards with further miming of the faces, and then asking the group to identify feelings that can be attributed to a face. Write down these feelings on the cards. The simple meal could take place at this point or after the first quick-think session, as appropriate.

The quick-think topic is: 'Why do children come to be "looked after" in foster care?' This could be threatening to members of the group and you may prefer to distance it for them by drawing either a boy or a girl on the flip chart and naming the child; entitle the session 'Why did Jade or Andrew come to be looked after?' Use the material for discussion, gently moving the discussion towards how Jade/Andrew might have felt. Encourage the use of the "feelings" words introduced earlier.

What Violet Oaklander calls a "fantasy trip" could follow. She suggests that relaxation exercises are useful before starting the work itself. We use several, for example:

Close your eyes. Starting with your toes, tense them. Gradually move up your body, tensing each muscle. Foot, shin, thigh and so on, right up to the head. Now let out all that tension slowly, feel it ebb away.

Then ask the group to close their eyes and take them on a fantasy trip. (This will lead to a drawing session, so have a supply of paper and colouring pencils ready.)

Let's pretend we're on an island. Take a walk through the island. Notice things: the colours of the flowers, the birds, the animals, fruit on the trees, the noises and smells. Suddenly, you enter a clearing and there is a big castle. Enter the courtyard. Walk across it. Enter the big hall. It is empty. You notice a staircase. Climb the stairs. At the top of the staircase there is a long corridor. You walk along it and you notice there are names on the doors. At the door with your name on it you stop. Enter the room. Have a good look round. Notice things. How does the room look? One last look around. Right, now open your eyes.

Now ask the group not to speak, but to draw a picture of what they saw in the room. The leaders can draw pictures too. When the pictures are ready, a leader asks individuals to share their drawings with them. Let the children describe the picture in their own words. Do not be tempted to interpret the picture back to them. Instead, for example, if a child has drawn a settee, you might ask what the settee is either thinking or feeling. What is it saying? We usually write down the child's comments on the drawing, encouraging the use of "feeling" words where this is appropriate.

Violet Oaklander believes that it is important to encourage children to share themselves. She regards it as a means of 'promoting the child's self discovery by asking him to elaborate on the parts of the picture. Making parts clearer, more obvious. Describing the shapes, forms, colours, representations, objects and people.'

You could finish off this session by playing a quiet game like "sleeping lions". Everyone stretches out on the floor and pretends to be a sleeping lion. One member, without physically touching anyone, attempts to get the others to move. He or she can pull faces, pretend to jump on a group member, blow on them, but must not touch anyone. Any movement or noise means that a person is no longer a sleeping lion and is therefore out of the game.

Session 3

Start with a group game, perhaps 'I went to market' once again. Have a quick-think session on: 'How might children feel about being in foster care?' and follow this up with discussion. Go on to a quick-think session on 'How did Jade/Andrew feel on her/his first day being looked after?' and follow this with role-playing about Jade/Andrew being looked after with the children playing different roles. The meal break might follow this, with the discussion continuing.

Another of Violet Oaklander's fantasy trips could then be introduced.

> *Close your eyes. Imagine you are a rose. What kind of rose bush are you? Are you very small? Are you large? Are you fat? Are you tall? Do you have flowers? If so, what kind? What are your stems and branches like? What are your roots like? Do you have any roots? Do you have leaves? What kind? Do you have thorns? Where are you? In a yard? In a park? In the desert? In the city? In the country? In the middle of the ocean?*
>
> *Are you in a pot, or growing in the ground, or through cement, or even inside somewhere? What's around you? Are there flowers or are you alone? Are there trees, animals, people, birds?*
>
> *Do you look like a rose bush or something else? Is there anything around you, like a fence; if so, what is it like? Or are you just in an open place?*
>
> *What's it like to be a rose bush? How do you survive? Does someone take care of you?*
>
> *What's the weather like for you right now?*
>
> *Open your eyes. Draw yourself as a rosebush.*

(Reproduced from Violet Oaklander's *Windows to our Children*)

Encourage the children to tell you about their drawings individually. Write on the drawing the thoughts and feelings of the rose bush. Do not be tempted to interpret the picture to the child.

Now is the time to introduce the idea of the life story book. First, quick-think the question: What are life story books? One group's contributions to the flipchart were:

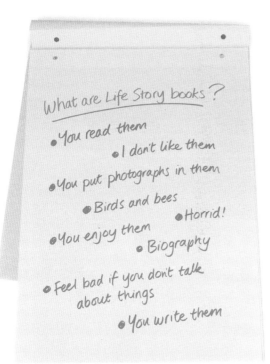

What are Life Story books?

- You read them
- I don't like them
- You put photographs in them
- Birds and bees
- Horrid!
- You enjoy them
- Biography
- Feel bad if you don't talk about things
- You write them

Use the material on the flipchart for discussion, acknowledging and accepting that making a life story book can be painful. Lead into how someone will be offering to make a life story book with each one of them. Finish this session with a quiet game.

Following this session, you should have a meeting with those who will be working individually on making a life story book with each child. The purpose is to share the broad outline of the group work, to explain how you have been using the material, and for mutual support. This meeting is particularly important if the child is displaying signs of regression.

Session 4

Open with a simple game. The work can be more loosely structured from now on. Sometimes we bring in a box of "play people" and glove puppets and wait for the children to take the lead. Frequently we have conversations between the dolls and puppets, talking about what they are thinking and feeling. This may lead to role-playing from something either a doll or a puppet has been "saying".

For another group activity, a leader has a large sheet of card on which he or she draws a shape, and then might say and write: 'This is me, in a red circle. I am all alone.' Someone else then draws a shape anywhere on the card, makes a comment and writes it down. (If we know that one of the group has difficulty with writing, one of the leaders takes responsibility for writing down all the comments.) The game continues until everyone has drawn at least two shapes.

Fit into the flow of the work any of these questions: 'What is a family? What is a foster family?' It is sometimes useful to return to earlier quick-think topics. The group's perceptions will change with time. Allow the children to express their feelings. If they make negative comments, do not try to persuade them differently. These topics usually raise fears about confidentiality. If so, reassure the group. You might lead on from this to a quick-think on 'Who can you trust?'

If there is time during the session, we use Vera Fahlberg's three parents model (see Chapter 8) to discuss how being looked after changes birth parents' rights and responsibilities, to reassure the children that no one is trying to take away what they were endowed with at birth and to explain the position of the foster carers.

Session 5

Open with 'I went to market' followed by a group game, such as 'You've done it again, Mabel'. In this game, players stand in a circle with one member in the centre. Another player jumps into the circle and says, 'You've done it again, Mabel, you've (for example) not paid the rent for five weeks'. The first person can either respond to this by explaining why 'Mabel has done it again' or admit that this is so by rejoining the circle. If 'Mabel' goes out, the accuser becomes the new 'Mabel' and another player jumps into the circle adding another accusation, 'You've done it again Mabel, you've...' and so the game continues, until everyone has had a turn or interest begins to wane. The group then breaks for a simple meal together.

Afterwards, we use a poem recommended by Violet Oaklander.* It was written by an eight-year-old Turkish girl and translated. Read it aloud while the group sits, eyes closed. (This poem can produce a powerful reaction, so you will have to try and gauge whether the group is ready for it.)

---

*Reproduced from 'Have you Seen a Comet?: Children's art and writing from around the world' (US Committee for Unicef: New York and the John Day Company).

There is a knot inside me

There is a knot inside me
A knot which cannot be untied
Strong
It hurts
As if they had put a stone
Inside of me
I always remember the old days
Playing at our summer house
Going to grandmother's
Staying at grandmother's
I want those days to return
Perhaps the knot will be untied when they return.
But there is a knot inside of me
So strong
It hurts
As if it is a stone inside of me

I'd Like to fly
I'd Like to but I can't
I wasn't meant to
But I want to
I was meant to be me

Why?
For some reason
I wish I was a bird to fly
and be free
I feel I am imprisoned

In anyway I am what
I am nobody can change
That or make that
But I wish

The group then draws pictures and the leaders talk to each child about their picture.

One 13-year-old girl wrote her own poem which we also sometimes use.*

You could suggest that they draw Jade/Andrew from Session 3 with their knot inside them. This could lead to discussion of how Jade/Andrew might tell the others in the residential unit how they feel inside.

By this stage in the life of the group you need to be sensitive to the issues the group might want to raise. For example, group members, especially if they are older children, might have experienced foster care breakdowns and may want to talk about this.

One group had a quick-think about the advantages and disadvantages of being in a foster home – see illustration.

At the end of the session close with a quiet, relaxing game.

Session 6

Open with a game. It could be a "scribble game" (from Violet Oaklander). Everyone stands with space around him or her. They close their eyes and pretend to scribble on a giant sheet of paper. Then they are each given paper and pens and close their eyes and reproduce this

Advantages and disadvantages
of being in a foster home

Advantages	Disadvantages
• Somewhere to go and live	• Break down
• Improves your life	• Ruins your life
• You like them	• Waste of time
• Better than your own home	• Isn't your own home

---

* *I'd like to fly*, Reproduced by kind permission of Angie.

scribble on their paper. When they open their eyes they try to identify the shapes produced.

From here they can go on to draw a picture of a time when they were laughed at. If this is too threatening, they can draw a time when Jade/Andrew was laughed at. Alternatively, they can take another fantasy trip in which a boat in a storm is described while the group sits, eyes closed. Then the group draws what they saw. The simple meal can be taken together after this.

Move on to a group story. We have some cards with pictures of houses, cars, a cat, a dog, an eagle, items of clothing and so on. We put a picture on the table and say something about it, for example, 'This is a house in a town'. The next person says something further about it, such as 'and the stick of dynamite came along to blow it up'. In one group someone put down a picture of a cat and added, 'Along came a lion and started to roar'. This was ridiculed by the group and used to discuss fantasising about things.

You could then go on to quick-think: 'How can we find foster families?' In dealing with this subject with older children, we try and help them understand how difficult it is to find substitute families for them. This can be discussed before the quick-think session and can be followed with a discussion about how to recruit substitute or foster families.

By this stage the children will be meeting their individual social workers and be working on life story books. We look at what they are doing and the ways that it might be of help in placement.

We might use role-playing here:

Foster carers being interviewed

Jade/Andrew's first visit to a new foster family

A problem which might arise in a foster family, like Andrew being caught smoking or Jade/Andrew being accused of stealing

We stop the role-play frequently in midstream and get the participants to change roles. We encourage them to talk about how it felt to be in the role. We stop the role-play and invite the group to say what a child's or foster carer's or social worker's secret voice might be saying inside them. If appropriate we use the candle technique (see Chapter 8) to complement the "three parents" from the earlier session.

We close as usual with a relaxing game.

Session 7

We use this session to illustrate how a life story book can be helpful by enlisting the help of an older child who has made one and has been in placement for some time. This child needs to feel secure and you will have to spend time with him or her assisting with the preparation. Towards the end of the session, the child's foster carers might be included in the discussion as well. If children have experienced a foster care disruption, they often interrupt the session to talk about their experiences and make comparisons.

JASON

Jason spoke to a group about his life. When he reached the part of his story where he met his birth mother for the first time, it produced a barrage of questions: 'What was it like?' 'Did you cry?' 'Did she cry?' 'Did you kiss each other?' Jason's reply stunned them. 'No, I didn't feel anything. It could have been someone in the street. I felt nothing.'

One child asked Jason how he had expected his mother to be. 'Tall and rich' was the wry reply. This, of course, vividly demonstrated how we all have fantasy pictures in our minds.

Frequently the group will use this session to talk about their feelings about their birth families. The group should close on a note of optimism as they understand how making a life story book to establish the past is helpful.

Session 8

This is the final session of the first phase and needs to be organised around the feelings of loss that will be felt by all. Open by talking about the previous session. Ask members to draw something they remember from it and use their drawings for discussion.

Have the simple meal together, with perhaps a special treat to mark the occasion. Go on to quick-think: 'What was this group about? What should be included in the next group for other children?' Follow with a quiet drawing session in which the members of the group might draw cards for each other. End with a quick-think on: 'How do we feel?'

There should be at least two follow-up group meetings at six-weekly intervals. Before they go, remind the group of this and that they will be meeting together again. Before the next meeting, get together with the children's individual workers to talk about the progress they are making with the life story work and to discuss the broad features of the group.

Session 9

This should be arranged about six weeks after the core group finishes. If substitute families have been found for some of the children, the focus can be orientated towards "bridging" work. Ideally, the leaders should have made contact at least once during the intervening six weeks. Send a letter about a week before the meeting to remind the child of the date, and suggest in it that they might like to bring along their life story book.

The session can be loosely structured around what you have done in earlier sessions. We find that many children are prepared to share their life story books with the group. This can lead to a discussion of the feelings invoked while making the books. Inevitably, expectations will have been aroused about substitute families. With older children these may not be fulfilled. The group will need to look at the reality of this and be helped to talk about their disappointment and frustrations. During the six-week interval before the next meeting, there will be further meetings with the children's individual social workers.

Session 10

The purpose of this session is to reinforce the skills acquired through the group meetings: the ability of the children to talk about their hopes, fears and pain. The focus of this meeting will depend upon what has happened or is about to happen in their lives. If some children are now in placement, sharing their experiences might be usefully explored. We have used material from the Fostering Network and CoramBAAF's training materials to give children some insight into how moving into a foster family can affect them. We have concentrated on that part of the material that confronts foster carers with the changes they will have to make. Frequently, children have not considered the fact that foster carers have to make adjustments too.

Ideally, there should be further meetings at intervals as a means of helping the group members to give mutual support to one another. Between these meetings there should be further discussion with the children's individual foster carers.

12 Working with children with a disability

Ann Atwell

At the time of writing, Ann Atwell was a Homefinder, Dumfries and Galloway Region Social Work Department.

Children with a disability have the same "child" needs as any other child, and this means having an accurate account of their personal history.

There can be a reluctance to become involved in life story work with children who have a disability, and those involved with these children need to examine their own feelings about this. One of the most common reasons is that some social workers are themselves quite uncomfortable with learning disabilities and may as a result avoid contact. It is important to recognise this and either accept it and not become involved in work with people with learning disabilities or undertake additional training to help overcome any difficulty. A second problem with undertaking this work is where the worker has difficulty in communicating with a disabled person, and is unable or unwilling to take time to learn how the disabled person most readily communicates. Thirdly, there is sometimes a wish to be overprotective of the disabled child, thus avoiding any work that has the potential to be upsetting or painful. Fourthly, there needs to be sensitivity towards the child's particular sensory modes and using those with which a child is comfortable (see *Every Child is Special* by Jenny Cousins, published by BAAF in 2006).

Another barrier to life story work is the continuing belief that families who would wish to take on a child with learning disabilities will not be found. This can lead to deferment of vital work until a family has been identified, which does not allow the disabled child space and time to internalise their own life history and grieve the loss of their birth family before moving to a new family.

How communication happens

One of the most common reasons for life story work not being undertaken is the belief that the young person's learning disabilities are too severe, therefore the work is pointless. But take the case of Fiona, aged 13.

FIONA

Fiona had severe learning disabilities as well as being physically disabled. She was the size of a three-year-old and spent most of her time stripped naked in her cot, having divested herself of all her clothing and bedding except for one cover under which she hid, sitting in the corner of her cot in the foetal position. She had only a few tufts of hair due to pulling it out in handfuls; her skin was bleeding and scarred from self-abuse through picking and biting it; she had frequent screaming tantrums and banged her head regularly. She could not walk or talk, and she resisted overtures by staff to get close and cuddle her. Because it was unclear how much she understood, the only life story work done was to talk to her regularly about where her family was and why she was in hospital, as well as about the plan to move her to a foster family. This produced no response from Fiona except her usual tantrums.

Once in placement, Fiona showed some ability to understand the world and to convey her wishes. For example, whenever the family went on a car trip to the nearby town where Fiona used to live, she recognised the town from the outskirts and became agitated and distressed. This happened on every occasion so could not be dismissed as coincidence. She also frequently had a tantrum as they were setting off on a car journey, but eventually settled down. Through time, the foster father wondered whether Fiona's tantrum was Fiona's way of reminding him to fasten his seat belt, which he normally didn't do until round the first corner from their house (about 50 yards). When this theory was tested out it proved to be the case. When the foster father "belted up" Fiona didn't have her usual tantrum. Both of these situations had previously been attributed to 'Fiona just having one of her tantrums' and only through keen observation was it realised that she was communicating. So one of the fundamental lessons of Fiona's story is not to assume that those with severe learning disabilities cannot communicate, but to question our own ability to understand how the communication is being made.

Where to begin is often seen as a problem, but understanding the child is fundamental and will dictate where and how to begin. For example, if a child is hyperactive and has poor concentration, it is perhaps pointless to consider traditional life story work, since the method of sitting and writing and drawing will be particularly difficult for a hyperactive child.

JOHN

John was such a child and instead of making a book, he made more sense of frequent repetitive tours round the area where he grew up, with visits to the family home and local shops, parks, etc, all of which were captured on video film. Even though John rarely watched television normally, he was captivated by seeing himself on TV along with people

and places recognisable to him, and he would watch this over and over again, telling anyone who cared to listen where and what the pictures were. Such a combination of methods, which includes physically visiting people and places of significance and recording them on video, combined to produce an understandable and readily accessible life story for John.

Doing life story work using a computer can be especially useful for children with a speech or hearing impairment.

There are a number of interactive CD-ROMs available for direct work with children. For example, *My Life Story* (Betts and Ahmad, 2003) *Speakeasy* (Betts, 2004), and *Billy and the Big Decision* (Information Plus, 2010) are packages that help professionals communicate with children about their experiences, views, wishes and feelings, including potentially distressing experiences such as illness and abuse. Children are willing to engage with these media and they can also help provide aesthetic distance.

In My Shoes is another computer package that can aid communication, and uses images, sound, speech and video. Through a series of modules, children are encouraged to share information on their experiences and emotions with different people in home, educational and other settings. The programme has been designed so that a trained adult will sit alongside the child and assist, guide and interact with them through a structured interview process. It is an excellent means of engaging the child and building rapport between the child and the interviewer.

Who should do life story work?

In deciding how to tackle life story work with disabled children, it is also important to consider who would be best able to do this work. Since being able to understand and communicate with the child is paramount, this should be undertaken by the person who communicates best with the child, rather than assume it is always done by the child's social worker. For example, a worker in a residential home may be the most significant as well as most trusted adult for the child. For some children who may previously have spent a considerable time at home, there will be a wealth of family knowledge still contained in the family that will be vital for the child's life story work. For example, they may be able to identify things from family life to include in a life story video or book. Sometimes there is a toy or family ornament that has a story attached to it or was a particular favourite, or sometimes a piece of music like a theme tune from a TV programme may have particular family significance. By incorporating such stimuli, it is easier to sustain the attention of the young person and help make connections.

Using different methods

For children with a disability who perhaps have difficulty in communicating by speech, or who may lack the use of one or more of the senses, it is possible to develop life story work that does not depend only on visual methods but involves stimulation of other senses.

AARON

For Aaron who was blind, much of his life story work was interspersed with tactile stimuli, for example, buttons from a favourite person's jacket, a shell from a seaside outing with the family, dried flowers from the garden. It also included a handkerchief perfumed with his birth mother's favourite perfume.

For a child such as Aaron, it is also more helpful to use audio rather than visual methods of life story work, and his written life story was also recorded on a phone. It is possible to convey a spoken message from the birth parent by this method, rather than the more traditional letter that some parents write to their child. This naturally would depend on how appropriate it was at that point to involve the parent to this degree. Positive involvement of the birth parent in this way, as in video life stories (you can record this on a smartphone), is possible. What greater stimulus could there be for a child than to hear the voice or see the face of their parent or another family member? Such work assumes co-operation by the birth family. Where the family has been through the painful process of relinquishing the child, it is often a helpful way of them being constructively involved in part of the child's future.

In contemplating life story work for a child who has a severe disability and who may have lived in an institutional setting for some years, one of the difficulties can be that the child has no understanding, or at best a very poor understanding, of "normal family life". Before helping such a child plan for a move to substitute family care, for example, it is necessary to find a method of life story work that helps the child understand the notion of "family" in the first place.

DARREN

Darren was such a boy, and by means of a cardboard pop-up house and cut-out people shapes, on to which were pasted the real photographic faces of family members and staff and children at the residential unit, some work was done to give Darren a sense of who belonged in which household. Since Darren's mother and brother were going to be significant people for him, and regular contact would continue in his new family placement, a further pop-up home was made to represent the new family. Their cut-outs were added to their pop-up house. It was

then possible to work over some sessions with Darren to convey that his birth mother and brother would spend time in the new house, as well as conveying to Darren that he would move from the residential unit to the new house and new family.

Some caution might be needed in adopting a "third object" approach to life story work, since this can sometimes complicate the task or confuse the child with learning disabilities who might not readily make a connection between, say, a puppet and him or herself, or a story about an animal. Far better to work with direct references and keep this as simple as possible and appropriate to that particular child's skills and abilities.

Even for a child who has only a mild to moderate disability, and who therefore may have writing and drawing skills, the traditional life story book may not necessarily be the preferred way to record the child's history. For example, if a child has writing and drawing skills but is not interested in sitting down to this sort of work and would rather be playing with computer games, it may be possible to engage the help of someone with computer skills who can computerise the child's history in a way that stimulates the child's interest. *Digital Life Story Work* (Hammond and Cooper, 2013) is a book which describes how to use technology, particularly computers, camcorders and smartphones, in a range of contemporary life story projects designed to engage the interest of older children and young people. (Chapter 14 provides an introduction to digital life story work).

In summary:

- don't be afraid to tackle this work;

- decide who is the best person to do the work;

- understand the child's means of communication;

- identify the child's skills and interests;

- construct a method or methods that take account of this.

13 Working with children who have been sexually abused

Gerrilyn Smith

Gerrilyn Smith is currently the National CAMHS Consultant for Advanced Child Care and a former clinical psychologist in child and adolescent mental health services.

To do life story work with children who have been sexually abused, you will need to adapt some of the skills and tasks already described in previous chapters. The sexual abuse of some of the children you will work with will be known about and may have resulted in their being removed from their families of origin. Work with these children is less problematic than with those children where sexual abuse in their family of origin has not been disclosed but there are indicators and/or suspicions that it is an issue.

Children known to have been sexually abused

It is important if you are working with a child where it is known that they have been sexually abused, that you acknowledge the abuse. This can save a lot of time in doing life story work. Many children in the care system do not know what other people know about them. They may not know if it is alright to talk about their past experiences. By raising the subject of sexual abuse early on, you are signalling to the child that you will talk about it with them. You may also want to know who else has talked about it with the child. If very little work has been done with the child about their experience of abuse, you need to prepare yourself for a longer task than you originally bargained for. Life story work should not replace therapy. The life story work should remain task-centred, recording important past experiences that they can keep. Talking with you now will make talking in therapy easier later on. It may be whilst doing life story work that it becomes clear to you or to the older child with whom you are working that further work needs to be done.

There are some important messages you need to convey to the child about their experience of sexual abuse.

Belief

It is important that you demonstrate your belief that it did happen. You may also want to explore why it is difficult for children to tell about sexual abuse, and to suggest that sometimes, after children have told, they remember other things about the abuse that they haven't told people. You need to let the child know it is okay to remember. You may also want to discuss why some children would prefer to forget or say it didn't happen when it did. You could make a list of people who believed the child and people who did not, including members of the child's family and extended family. This can help a child understand why they are no longer living with their family of origin. If their original family did not believe sexual abuse had happened, it will be impossible for them to protect the child in the future.

Defining right and wrong

You need to offer some comments about the rights and wrongs of sexual abuse that are developmentally appropriate, for example: 'It is right for children to tell adults. It is wrong for adults to sexually abuse children.' These may be important messages to give to those children who are showing signs of sexual bullying, or who are clearly sexually offending against other children. You may need to show that you understand why a child might sexually offend against other children, but that a history of sexual victimisation is not an excuse to do it to others.

What happened?

It may be useful to record from the child's point of view what happened when they told. What did their mum say or do? What about their dad? Their brothers and sisters? It can be helpful to record what the child would have liked to have happened. This is important as it not only identifies and records what did happen, but also provides the child with a model response that can inform both their current carers and the child as a future parent.

If the child is looked after and the offender is still in the family, the child may have strong feelings that they are being punished for telling. Be honest about the unfairness of the situation: it is unfair that children are deprived of their family because an adult won't own up to having a serious problem. You may be able to identify whom the child would like to have contact with and what might be safe circumstances under which contact could occur. Many of the other tasks and suggestions identified in this book can be used with children who have been sexually abused. You need to be prepared for the confusions they will express if no one has talked about the meaning of their abuse with them before.

Children who have been sexually abused can have both positive and negative feelings about the perpetrators. Reinforce whatever feelings they have. If they have no positive feelings that is OK. The same is true for a child who has no negative feelings. Avoid making assumptions about how the child should feel about the perpetrator or other members of their family. It can be useful to recognise and record that this is how they feel right now. This leaves room for the child to change how they feel at a future date.

Some children who have been sexually abused may not be ready to do life story work when you are. This may be because remembering their past abuse is too traumatic for them and makes them feel worse. They could experience flashbacks during the sessions. Workers should therefore go at the pace of the child. If the child is clear they do not feel able to talk about the abuse in more detail at this time you should let them know that is okay. You should help the child understand why acknowledging the sexual abuse is important for the adults who will be caring for him or her in the future. It may be sufficient to record something like: '"X" was touched by her dad in ways she didn't like. She doesn't feel able to talk about it now but maybe she will in the future.'

You can still make comments indicating your belief, and your position on the moral issues surrounding what happened. You could even speculate about what the child might like to have happened.

If you use euphemisms for sexual abuse, select one that the child has used or feels comfortable with. There is no need for explicit detail about what happened. A life story book can help teach a child the difference between private and public and how to present this. Many children I see for therapy bring their life story books with them to one of the early sessions as a way of introducing themselves to me.

Undisclosed sexual abuse

If a child has not disclosed sexual abuse but it is suspected, workers may wish to suggest to the child that they or other professionals were worried that the child had been sexually abused. Before doing this, the workers need to feel assured that the child is safe (i.e. not currently being abused) and to know what their agency procedures are in the event of a clear disclosure. If this is likely to require investigation by a primary investigation team, then the worker will need to tell the child what will happen next and why it needs to be followed up. If the child discloses abuse in their family of origin and they currently reside elsewhere but still have contact with their family of origin, you will need to consider how to manage the future contact. It may be appropriate to consider cancelling it until a more detailed assessment can be made. If a child discloses abuse in their current placement, this will need to be investigated by a primary investigation team. It is important that you explain this to the child, as they may need to be moved.

Sometimes a child makes a partial disclosure. He or she may tell about being sexually abused but not identify the perpetrator. You can still carry on with life story work incorporating the issues raised above, perhaps speculating as to why it is hard for the child to identify who sexually abused them.

Conclusion

This is only a brief summary of issues to consider in doing life story work with children who have been sexually abused. Children do disclose new abuse when doing life story work. This may be because it provides the child with space to reflect on their past experiences, or the focus of the task makes it possible for the child to talk about it, in a way that therapy or counselling did not.

If it becomes clear that more work needs to be done or that the life story work is triggering traumatic memories that impede the child's normal development, referral for therapy should perhaps be considered and life story work suspended until the child is more emotionally secure in the present, rather than traumatised by the past and any mention of it. Workers need to be familiar with their agency's policy and procedures and understand where life story work fits in, especially when dealing with new disclosures of information that raise further child protection issues.

14 Digital life story work in action

Simon P Hammond

Dr Simon P Hammond is a Research Fellow at the University of East Anglia (UEA). His work in this area began following his time as a residential worker. Simon was interested in how young people were using digital technologies to communicate with those around them and sought ways to enable the positive use of these tools when working with young people. Simon is committed to translating research into practice and works with a range of care providers to achieve this – see www.digitallifestorywork.co.uk for more details.

Introduction

With the rapid and continued spread of digital technologies, practitioners are starting to use digital media, such as computers and smartphones, in life story work. Digital life story work, as it is known, can provide exciting new opportunities for supportive conversations with young people that can help them to make sense of their past, understand their experiences and help develop their aspirations for the future. Digital media can be used in this work with children of all ages, but is most often employed with young people. This chapter focuses on work with this age group.

The use of digital tools to communicate with looked after young people has been mentioned in previous influential works (Fahlberg, 1994; Ryan and Walker, 2007). However, the use of these tools in frontline practice is still not widespread (Ahmad *et al*, 2008; Tregeagle and Darcy, 2008; Hammond, 2009; Hammond and Cooper, 2013). This chapter explores the benefits of using digital media with young people, and shows how technology can be used in simple, fun and imaginative ways. It also details points to be considered before starting work. Like the four-year research project that informs it, this chapter is underpinned by real-world practice experiences of using digital media with looked after young people. Numerous interviews and focus groups with young people and carers were undertaken during this project, and provide quotes and case study examples of digital life story work in action.

The chapter provides an overview of some of the areas covered in *Digital Life Story Work: Using technology to help young people make sense of their experiences* (Hammond and Cooper, 2013). This book, written by myself and Neil Cooper, provides a comprehensive guide on how to use computers, free software, smartphones and camcorders in a series of fun and engaging projects and is worth consulting for those wishing to dig deeper into this subject. The book also features a range of "projects", providing a step-by-step guide from a technological and practice perspective.

Why "digital" life story work?

Life story work with younger children uses a range of conventional approaches such as drawing, using glove puppets and "feelings faces". I do not claim that older children do not enjoy activities such as making collages and drawing, but conventional life story work resources are designed to appeal to younger children and tend to be led by the practitioner. This is understandable – life story work is primarily used to assist younger children's preparation for moves into long-term living arrangements. Unfortunately this emphasis means that life story work can be viewed by professionals, carers and young people as something to be "done in childhood". For adolescents (who are often very aware of how they are seen by others, engaging in activities "for kids" or that are "done in childhood") the prospect of undertaking life story work is unlikely to be very appealing. This can present a barrier for practitioners seeking to engage adolescents in reflective conversations about their identity.

Young people are often portrayed as the pioneers of digital technologies. We often talk about adolescents as "digital natives" – those born into a digital age – as opposed to "digital immigrants" – those of us for whom such technologies are "new" rather than how things have always been. Digital life story work encourages professionals to make use of this common perspective. Digital life story work projects seek to empower young people to make use of the everyday accessible digital technologies that many appear glued to. In this way, digital life story work capitalises on the ways in which adolescents choose to communicate with each other and those around them.

Ideas for doing digital life story work

Digital life story work projects can be small or large, simple or complex. By engaging initially in smaller, simpler projects, practitioners and young people can build their skills and confidence for undertaking more complex work. What the project will involve can be decided in discussion with the young person, depending on their interest, the practitioner's and young person's goal for the work, and what resources are available. The resources needed will vary – a computer, camcorder, and various software (often available free) can all be useful, but a vast amount can be accomplished with just a smartphone.* A strength of this approach is that it encourages the young person to use the very technology they may already own and have access to, emphasising ownership over the process and materials (or products) created.

---

* The following link from the BBC's Click programme provides an example of what can be done with smartphone technology and downloadable applications: http://news.bbc.co.uk/1/hi/programmes/click_online/9710004.stm

Digital life story work can – and should – be engaging, exciting and imaginative. Some initial ideas for work with young people are detailed below:

- **Remaking memories:** As well as helping to keep valuable photos safe, the process of scanning, editing and embellishing photos provides an opportunity for discussion and reflection.

- **Making audio recordings:** The young person can choose stories from their life that they would like to record, or could choose to interview, or be interviewed by, the practitioner or other people in their lives.

- **Soundscapes:** By recording sounds from their current or previous everyday environments, young people can creatively tell stories or illustrate their feelings.

- **Photo mash up:** Using online software, the young person can be helped to create collages to illustrate relationships between different photos, or to explore complex family situations.

- **Making a digital comic strip:** Short, simple cartoons can help the young person express their feelings, illustrate their past life, and address emotions that might be difficult to articulate in discussion with another person.

- **Making short video logs (vlogs):** The process of movie-making can help young people to reflect on their past and present, as well as providing a record of how they thought and felt at a point in time.

- **Podwalks:** Building on short movies, Podwalks involve filming while engaging young people as "tour guides", showing the worker(s) around places of importance to them whilst sharing stories linked to those places. This is more complex and potentially emotional work, but can be particularly engaging and helpful for the young person.

- **Virtual Podwalks:** For occasions when physically revisiting a place of importance is not possible, the use of free software such as Google Maps or Google Earth allows people to visit places from a birds-eye or street level view (as shown below).

Many of these projects (which are covered in greater detail in Chapter 2 of Hammond and Cooper, 2013) will create a finished digital product, which should be kept securely and can be celebrated by, for instance, holding a premiere for a short movie. However, the most important point of the work is of course the supportive relationship shared between the practitioner and young person. This is an opportunity for the young person to be supported in thinking and reflecting about their lives, feelings and experiences.

How can digital media add value to life story work?

It is important to keep in mind that, in and of themselves, there is nothing special about digital technologies. They are not a "magic wand" that removes complexity and provides an immediate solution as to how to engage adolescents in reflective, therapeutic conversations. They do not automatically bestow reflective qualities on those who use them. They are simply engagement tools, albeit very appealing and powerful ones for young people.

Capturing the process

Like conventional life story work, there are two broad elements to any digital life story work project – "process" and "product". The products, discussed later in this chapter, are the items created as a result of engaging in the process. In conventional life story work, an example product would be a life story book. The therapeutic process involves creating opportunities to open up conversational spaces. These spaces provide young people with opportunities to share accounts of their own lives, in their own words. These accounts are listened to by a consistently available adult who can sensitively support the young person's reflections on the stories they choose to share, and potentially, provide re-scripting or re-editing advice.

Unlike traditional life story work, using digital media provides ways of capturing, editing and re-editing young people's stories, as well as the therapeutic relationship context (i.e. the process) experienced at the point in time in which the work was undertaken. Photos, music and film can help illustrate the young person's life and relationships in dynamic, imaginative ways that traditional methods cannot. This also enables representations of the relationships experienced at a certain point in time to be stored for posterity.

Having a representation of this relationship is an important aspect that can be easily overlooked. Imagine telling a story to someone you do not know about a person they do not know, in a place they have never been and are unlikely to ever go. Telling such a story is challenging – it involves a great deal of description about the characters before the story can be told. This challenge becomes slightly easier with a photo, and easier still with a film clip that can show elements about people, places and the narrator's relationship with each. Appearances, accents, colloquialisms and mannerisms can be shown and the story narrated much more easily.

Considering the number of transitions young people can experience and relationships that end without the ability to call on individuals to help retell events, digital life story work can provide richer starting points. It is from these starting points that young people can begin to share and reinterpret stories of their past more readily than via conventional methods of representing supportive relationship contexts.

In undertaking projects involving multimedia/film recordings, "outtakes" are likely. These are a great way to allow the stories and relationships behind the projects to be kept for sharing accounts of the process of digital life story work projects.* The following case study illustrates the importance of the story behind the story.

THE STORIES BEHIND THE STORIES

Jaiden (15) took part in a digital life story work project that involved him recording short (at least two minutes long) video log (vlog) entries over a period of six months. Following the end of the project, the vlog entries were transferred onto a DVD and memory stick for him to keep. With Jaiden's permission, a copy of the DVD was also given to his carer for safe keeping.

After recording his vlogs, Jaiden would frequently record spoof vlog entries. This involved a variety of inventive scenarios, with his favourite being his "Worldwide News" broadcasts. This involved Jaiden and me appearing in front of the webcam together and improvising news stories. A regular feature of Jaiden's spoof recordings was an update on my receding hairline. I would respond by providing an update, before 'throwing back to the studio' and asking for an update on when the council were coming back to finish cutting Jaiden's hair with their hedge trimmers.

Learning points: **Making oneself vulnerable by entering a young person's world can promote anxiety and self-consciousness, regardless of one's age. In digital life story work, in which young people can benefit from being in front of as well as behind the lens, it is an important step. If you are not willing to appear physically or verbally on the recording if invited, why would the young person? As in the earlier case study (and one might argue most relationships experienced in social care settings), the relationship between Jaiden and myself had an expiry date, a point in time at which Jaiden and I would no longer be in contact. By inviting me to be involved in his spoof news shows, Jaiden had a memento of the interpersonal relationship that he and I shared during the project, a memento that might help him explain one day about the time some bald lad from a local university asked him to take part in a research study.**

* This clip from Children's Liver Disease Talk Tell Transform residential programme offers an insight into this aspect: https://www.youtube.com/watch?v=45tUVZLW5jY

Digital life story work does not have to concentrate on large, dramatic events in young people's lives (although it may be used in this way). Many everyday things in life can move from mundane to meaningful once they stop. This could be a young person's bedroom or their changing physical features. The following case study is taken from the original four year long research project (see Hammond, 2012) and illustrates how the line between mundane and meaningful is linked to time, and how digital media can create digital time capsules.

MUNDANE TO MEANINGFUL

Lynk (16) and Abby (14) took part in a digital life story work project similar to that undertaken by Jaiden above.

Lynk recorded his vlog entries in the dining room of his foster home. He would often talk about his week, including what he had done at the weekend, going or not going to his education placement and what he wanted to do on the forthcoming weekend. Lynk would record his vlog in front of me (author and researcher who acted as facilitator for the project), who would sit at the opposite end of the dining table. Lynk would then invite me to watch the vlog with him. At the end of the project, Lynk and I watched all the clips together, with Lynk enjoying seeing how much he had physically changed. This led to conversations about who he took after in his family and wider conversations about family life.

Abby (14) alternated between recording her vlog entries in the living room and bedroom of her foster home. I would often be "sent out" when she recorded her vlogs, before being asked to watch them with her. Whilst recording one in her bedroom, she provided a tour of this room. This included posters on her bedroom door, her shoes, her DVD player, and photos of members of her birth family as well as hand-drawn Rest In Peace (RIP) posters for her granddad, aunty and uncle, and a poem given to her by her birth mother. In re-watching these clips, Abby spoke about her changing living circumstances during the project.

Learning points:

For young people in care, who can often lack consistently available adults to help them reflect about how much they have changed or about what their previous placements were like, recordings from young people's everyday lives can become more meaningful as time passes and/or circumstances change. Creating digital time capsules of everyday life helps preserve the "mundaneness" of everyday living situations and allows meaning to be created when they are watched and stories are told and retold by young people.

A central part of any life story work is the relationship shared during the undertaking of the work, and this is the same for digital media. Having a consistently present adult facilitator who is able to gently guide the young person to reorder/fill in gaps in stories by jogging their memory with reflective questions is crucial. This person also needs to be a role model, particularly when handling the inherent frustrations of working with digital media in innovative ways and helping to mediate the risks that digital media may bring (discussed later in this chapter). This individual also needs to be the young person's audience and a compassionate listener. As Baynes (2008) highlights, those working with young people need to 'enter the young people's world'. In relation to digital life story work, this involves being aware that you may be invited to "appear" in shot with the young person. This may be uncomfortable for some, but it is important to remember that in undertaking this work you are a vital part of the process, the story behind the stories shared during the project, and someone likely to be remembered by the young person. This is of course a balance that needs to be negotiated on a case-by-case basis as these are, after all, the young person's stories and projects. However, it is important that you are aware that the young person may see you as a very important supporting cast member.

Editing, presenting and celebrating the products of digital life story work

In life story work, the creation or updating of a physical product, perhaps a life story book or memory box of some sort, provides a tangible end product. Digital life story work also has products – perhaps a photo collage, soundtrack or short film. Thanks to the range of computer programmes and applications available, these products are often aesthetically appealing to the young person (although of secondary importance to the process and relationship created and/or strengthened by undertaking the work). However, for the practitioner, being involved in the creation of a product that the young person likes is useful in promoting engagement with the process and empowering young people's ownership over the product(s) and the stories shared.

Digital material can be quickly and repeatedly edited and presented in an appealing manner – a particular strength. For example, in the case of a Podwalk, the ability to re-order sequences of film chronologically can be particularly beneficial, given the structural importance of temporal coherence within biographical stories.

In presenting the work, a common feature of free video editing software is the ability to quickly add cinematic appeal. With software, you can create DVD title screens, integrate digital photos, overlay writing on elements and add a soundtrack based on the young person's choice of music (discussed in more detail in Chapter 6 of Hammond and Cooper, 2013). This appealed to the young people in our project and became one of the most satisfying elements.

Screenshot showing an example of a DVD title menu

The aesthetic appeal of the products of digital life story work also poses a dilemma. The greater the aesthetic appeal, the greater the temptation to display it on social media (such as Facebook and Twitter). Creating an aesthetically pleasing product that can be shared requires consideration of who will view this product and, crucially, its content. Like all of us, looked after young people edit stories depending on the audience. The story of a night out is likely to be different when told to a close friend as opposed to a line manager. Therefore, it is important to keep in mind the remit of the digital life story work project and its end goals for each party. For the practitioner, a goal could be to assist a young person to come to terms with a variety of traumatic early life experiences. However, for the young person, a goal may be sharing a cool film clip with their friends. It is important to discuss what to share and what not to share, both at the start of and during the project. This also underlines the usefulness of film "outtakes", which can involve less sensitive material and therefore could be potentially shared more widely.

It is also important to remember that conversations "behind the scenes" when the equipment is not recording, i.e. the process, should support more sensitive reflections upon traumatic aspects of shared stories. Young people may choose to share reflections of these events on camera or they may not. Either way, the relationship continues to support reflections on these stories just as conventional life story work does. This also opens up dialogues for supporting young people to discriminate between appropriate and inappropriate personal boundaries and for conversations around the sorts of stories shared and mechanisms for sharing.

The digital challenge

> ...the more you ban it the more you, you go on it on your phone...you can't get away from it...

> (Becky, residential worker)

There can be risks to using digital media in life story work, and an awareness of these is important. Among practitioners, there is an understandable degree of nervousness around the promotion and usage of digital media in practice. Vulnerable young people can often struggle to maintain and discriminate between appropriate and inappropriate personal boundaries. On some occasions, this may result in too much being shared with those who may do them harm, and often too little with those trying to help. The same vulnerabilities can be amplified in online worlds where instant connections and personal communication are the norm. Young people may be geographically isolated but they are, thanks to these technologies, remotely connected.

However, as well as bringing some risks, digital life story work may stimulate conversations that allow young people to become more resilient in an ever-increasing digital world.

Managing personal digital boundaries

Kids don't need protection; we need guidance. If you protect us, you are making us weaker. We don't go through all the trial and error necessary to learn what we need to survive on our own...
(A quote from a child which features in *Safer Children in a Digital World,* Byron, 2008)

The ability to access the internet is no longer restricted to desktop computers, which may be fairly easily controlled, if necessary, by not letting young people use them. Today, we can go online from many different devices and locations. We do have web-filtering technologies to help block access to sites deemed inappropriate. However, relying on web filters to help safeguard young people online is unlikely to cover all the devices a young person may have access to (at home, at school, with friends, etc). The most important thing is to do more to openly engage, educate and empower vulnerable young people to develop their own digital resilience (Byron, 2008, 2010; Office for Standards in Education, Children's Services and Skills (OfSTED), 2010; Telenor Group, 2013; Hammond and Cooper, 2015; National Society for the Prevention of Cruelty to Children (NSPCC, 2015). By working with young people regularly via digital media, opportunities for conversations that seek to support "digital resilience" development are plentiful.

Anyone of any age can post anything they want online, and...come to regret it. Once posted, the content is "out there". Although content can be deleted, this does not mean that it has not been saved elsewhere or copied by others, as the NSPCC's #ShareAware campaign highlights. This has been made more instant and simpler via the integration of smartphones and a growing range of social media applications such as Facebook, Twitter, YouTube, Ask.fm, FMyLife, Flickr, WhatsApp, Snapchat, Skype, Pinterest, Tumblr and Instagram. Even users of Snapchat (an app which lets users send audiovisual content to another user that disappears after a number of seconds), who upload content that they expect to disappear shortly after viewing, need to be aware that there are numerous ways around this feature. Newer dating apps aimed at young people, such as Snog, MyLOL and Tinder's community for young people aged 13-17, heighten anxiety around young people coming into contact with explicit material. With the advent of live streaming applications such as Periscope, which enables users to watch and broadcast live video from all across the globe, this potential issue is further emphasised. Increased accessibility and the instantaneous nature of these apps underline the need for younger users to be supported to develop their own digital resilience.

When undertaking digital life story work with young people, and helping to support them in digitalising sensitive aspects of their lives, the capacity for them to share content with a wider audience is but a few clicks or swipes away. This is a common risk of digital life story work, emphasising the need for the relationship between you and the child to be supportive, reflective and advisory. The following case study, which features in Hammond and Cooper (2013), illustrates this point.

SHARING STABILISERS: "...A BIT TOO PERSONAL FOR FACEBOOK..."

Kai (15) took part in a digital life story work project that involved her scanning in old photos. In scanning old photos of herself and a birth family member, Kai was flicking between her Facebook profile and the task. Despite discussions advising her otherwise, she was determined to post one particular photo onto her Facebook profile. Over several hours, the photo attracted several unwanted comments, resulting in Kai becoming very upset, responding to comments and ultimately removing the picture. Unfortunately, the picture reappeared in other users' profiles, attracting similar derogatory comments. Kai was advised to "unfriend" and block these users. In working with Kai and discussing her feelings around these comments, it was decided that it would be best to upload the photos to a digital photo frame for Kai to keep in her room. After she had had time to reflect, Kai commented that: 'The old pictures I'd like put on here...(the photo frame) 'cos they're, um, a bit too personal for Facebook'.

Learning points:

Kai owned the original photo and had a copy of its reproduction. It was clear from conversations that if she was prevented from posting it on Facebook in-house, she would upload it regardless and that attempts to prevent her from doing so would lead to her relationship with staff and Simon becoming distant and less open. It was decided that, on balance, the relationship would be needed if and when negative/unwanted comments were received. Like riding a bike, we all learn from our mistakes and need support and guidance to do so. In this context, it was important that the supportive relationships were available to comfort, support and guide future actions. Although this was a risk, the risk of Kai dealing with these emotions without the support of the relationship was much more serious.

A fundamental criticism of digital life story work is that it may increase the risk of a young person posting personally sensitive content online, and the case study of Kai is a prime example. A more extreme example could be a young person posting a vlog entry online for, potentially, the whole world to see. However, as with events that are deemed safeguarding risks offline, the relationship offers a context in which opportunities to learn and support the young person are ample and need to be used.

Take, for example, preparing a meal with a young person who self-harms. Precautions may include discreetly counting in and out the sharp implements. Yet by preparing a meal, the risk of self-harming was increased. Later, if the young person was found to be self-harming, you would need to talk openly with them about self-harm, including when, why and how they do it, how they can clean and care for any injuries, as well as suggesting and exploring alternative coping techniques. The same is true of the case study featuring Kai and her posting of a photo online. The media may have changed, but the need for an understanding and supportive relationship has not.

Being involved in digital life story work projects opens up possibilities for wider discussions regarding the responsible use of digital media by young people. These purposeful conversations become embedded within the work itself. This should perhaps not be surprising as the way in which webpages are written encourages users to have multiple websites or "tabs" open. During digital life story work, young people are likely to want to be logged onto their various social media websites of choice. Whilst it may be possible to disable the internet on the computer being used for digital life story work in order to encourage focus on the task at hand, in some cases this may not be possible or desirable. This may provide opportunities to talk about the young person's use of social media and what it means to them. This can, in turn, of course open up conversations about how and what they use this for and how they do or do not protect their personal details.

Embracing powerlessness: the wider benefits of digital life story work

One of the key findings of the four-year research project was the way in which some workers embraced the powerlessness they felt in an effort to create opportunities to support the young person's resilience development. Workers realised that the young person's use of digital media was unlikely to stop because they and their organisations deemed it to be a safeguarding risk. Attempts to reduce access to digital media were also realised to be pointless, with the greater free availability of such technology. If a young person was determined to get on the internet, they would, regardless of whether this was supported or not.

By accepting that they were for all intents and purposes powerless to prevent the risks associated with internet use via controlling access alone, some workers were able to embrace the powerlessness and utilise it in positive ways (see Hammond and Cooper, 2013). Effectively, these workers took an "If you can't beat them, join them" stance towards young people's use of digital media, and focused instead on finding ways to support young people in online environments as opposed to trying to stop access. An example of this was that some homes set up their own Facebook profiles. Though profiles primarily set out to monitor young people's Facebook posts, they became much more. In one case, the profile attracted former residents to add them as friends and enabled staff to encourage peer-learning, where one resident assisted another in setting up their profile and negotiating privacy settings. By accepting and promoting the use of digital media, new opportunities to engage with a technologically proficient generation of young people can be created.

In the short term it is appealing to avoid all risk, but of course the world does not work like this. As with individuals who self-harm, or indeed those who wish to post inappropriate content online, in the longer term it is much better that the young person has a safe, supportive relationship context. In this way they can begin to address the underlying factors that trigger risky behaviours so they can be helped to self-regulate. Otherwise, as the child in the Byron report highlights, we risk making young people weaker. We need to create opportunities to support the young person to become empowered to help themselves, and support and coach them to get back on the bike when they fall, as one day they will be riding solo. Digital life story work offers limitless opportunities to have these conversations with young people.

Legacies of digital life story work

We've got to get used to this sort of technology, it isn't going anywhere.

(Holly, residential home manager)

In undertaking digital life story work with young people, technical skills are developed and shared which can provide a greater understanding of how technology can be used to assist with reflection, memories and self-understanding. This know-how enables ongoing work and equips young people with ways of thinking and reflecting that may be utilised throughout their lives.

Some elements of digital life story work material will be created to enable the young person to grow in maturity, and some material will be "left behind" as the conversations around its creation or the work become forgotten over time. Some things that feel significant as you create them may be left unregarded on the computer. Of course, the materials are not finished products or simply evidence of such work being undertaken, but are the vehicle for conversations around the young person's life experiences, current circumstances and future aspirations. As young people move on to other avenues of expression and communication, the partnership working through digital life story work can be continued as the young person moves into other phases of life. As we change and mature, we reflect and transform how we see things in our lives. It can be useful to go over material that was created early in the digital life story work process to provide an opportunity to discuss how things have changed and how new perspectives have formed. Looking over materials can illustrate complexity and contradictions that might not have been so easy to see when the material was first generated. Some material that appeared fun to develop may evoke new emotions when revisited.

Undertaking digital life story work also equips practitioners with a range of opportunities to add value to this therapeutic exercise. As well as the usual benefits associated with life story work, the flexibility of digital content enables further use and celebration with young people. This can take many forms, limited only by the imagination of the young person and adult facilitator. Digital life story work products can be copied easily and, with permission, back-up copies can be stored with young people's files for posterity.

In relation to the wider benefits of digital life story work, it is important not to underestimate how many activities important for everyday living now take place online. Current and future generations of care leavers will transition into a world in which many tasks of independent living, such as money management, paying utility bills and purchasing everyday goods can happen via smartphones. These portals of communication are playing a more prominent role in everyday lives beyond the care system. We need to ensure that we are proactive in promoting opportunities for digital resilience to develop and continue to equip our young people with these wider key living skills.

Conclusion

Globally, it is fair to say that the social care sector has been reactive rather than proactive in using digital ways of communicating in work with young people. However, this is starting to change and attract more interest. Work in Denmark around developing a 'MySocialWorker' application, which links social workers and young people, is ongoing (Mackrill *et al*, 2015). In Australia, Barnardo's has developed a cloud-based guided practice case management system, 'MyStory', which enables the documentation of a child/young person's life story in a secure digital memory box. In the UK, the 'Mind of my Own' consultation and advocacy application (www.mindofmyown.org.uk) and my own work on the Memorify™ digital life story work service also offer potentially fruitful ways forward. As the importance of digital technologies continues to grow, hopefully our embrace of these technologies and their imaginative possibilities in life story work will flourish as well.

15 Using life story work in rehabilitating children to their families

Alison Horrox, Emma Hall, Rodger Walker

Alison Horrox is a full time foster carer who has a great deal of experience in working with children to carry out Life Story Work. She also delivers training to other foster carers to feel confident in carrying out this vital work.

After several years working for inclusive and child centred practice for Looked After Children, Emma Hall is now studying to become a primary school teacher to further her passion for equal opportunities and tailored learning for all children within education.

One of the benefits of doing life story work is that it produces lots of information about why children are behaving as they do and how they view their original families. The process of talking to children about what they think happened when they were with their families, and how they came to be separated from them, tells us a lot about how they see their parents and siblings and how they are likely to act when they return to them.

Sharing this information with their family and discussing with them the best way of helping their child to adjust to being back with them can speed up the process of successful rehabilitation and reduce the stress on the child and their family at the same time. If the child's family can be involved in the life story work, the child can also learn how the family sees them and how they saw the process of separation. This can be a revelation to the returning child who may well have constructed an explanation of what happened based on them being solely at fault or based on a demonisation of their family. Children rarely understand the inexorable processes that can disrupt families or that their parents can fail without being evil.

The parents themselves can benefit from being involved in life story work because it is often the first time they can tell their side of the story away from the adversarial atmosphere of the court and in a way which they feel will help their child. Sometimes it can help them explain their own lives to themselves and their child.

Children usually have a cover story, mostly constructed by themselves, which explains to themselves and others why they are in care and which often makes heroes of their parents (who will return soon and rescue them from care) or demonises one or other of their parents or their siblings. These cover stories are usually factually inaccurate and unless clarified can cause problems later.

One young person cared for by one of the authors of this article firmly believed that the reason she was in care was because her mother had died of cancer and that her older siblings abandoned her to the care system. This was damaging to her self-esteem (she wasn't worth being "saved" by her siblings) and prevented her from being in contact with her siblings. After doing life story work she learnt that her mother and father had been inadequate parents long before the onset of her mother's cancer and that her siblings had tried hard to keep her but were defeated by inadequate support from Children's Services. She resumed contact with her siblings which helped her sense of identity greatly and also gave her a resource for the future.

What follows is the description of an example of the use of life story work by his foster carer in the process of rehabilitation for John, a looked after child, for whom the plan was that he return to live with his mother after several years of separation during which he had lived with his paternal grandparents and then his father.

JOHN

At the time described here, John was 12 years old, and was in care on a voluntary basis after a house fire, following which John and his mother were left homeless. Part of his cover story was that his mother had given him to his paternal grandparents because she did not love him enough and had more or less forgotten him. John believed that he had always lived with his grandparents and that his mother had "hurt him" by throwing him from an upstairs window. In August 2013, the police were called to John's grandparents' house on an unrelated matter and found that the house was unfit for a child to be living there and he was removed immediately. John had originally been placed with his father, but his father felt he could not cope with his behaviour. The plan for John was to be moved to a residential unit, but his mother asked to be considered to have him return to live with her. It was decided that she should be assessed to see if this would be possible.

In the interim, John was placed with a foster carer from an independent fostering agency who was experienced in life story work. His local authority agreed that life story work would help the rehabilitation plan and that the foster carer could carry out this work as only she had the resources and time to carry out life story work with children placed for rehabilitation. The local authority allowed access to John's files which provided the carer with the information to assess the accuracy of John's cover story, and a support worker from the fostering agency was appointed to help with the work. John's mother, Stacey, was asked if she would be a part of the life story work as the foster carer believed that John was confused about why he was living with his grandparents and why he didn't see his mother. She agreed to be a part of the sessions and she was asked to collect anything she had relating to John's early life, such as photographs or pictures he might have made. Stacey agreed to

this and set about collecting evidence relating to John's early life with her.

The life story sessions took place every two to three weeks for five months. Initially they took place at the offices of the agency but, once established, they took place at the foster carer's home, which allowed John the option of leaving the sessions to go to his room for periods of time if he needed to. In between sessions, John and his mother were able to talk to each other and the foster carer about what had been discussed and any new questions that came up could be answered without necessarily waiting for the next meeting. The support worker who was involved with the work was able to research anything that John or Stacey wanted more information about, such as which schools he had attended and when he had been there, and she took photographs of where John was born and the houses he had lived in, as well as finding information about the town he came from and his wider family. She was also able to offer John some space on his own to discuss any issues or concerns he had arising from the sessions with someone who was slightly removed from the situation.

Working with John

In the first meeting, we developed a timeline of significant events that had taken place in his life, as this was an invaluable way to show John a visual representation of what had happened to him and where his mother had fitted in to it. Stacey was able to tell him stories about him as a baby as well as give him facts about his birth weight, how long she was in labour and when he started to walk and talk, none of which he had known. His grandparents and father were asked to contribute, but they declined.

The next sessions involved us working through the information we had gathered and putting it into chronological order, whilst discussing in depth any issues that John or Stacey wanted to address. In this way, we were able to ensure that important events were covered, but allow John to dictate the pace and content of our discussions, and ask the questions that he most wanted answering.

At the end of each session, a plan was formulated about what would happen next: what other information was still needed and when and where the next session would take place. The sessions were recorded on feedback sheets that were given to John's social worker to document the progress being made. They were also as a demonstration of John's and his mother's commitment to the work and were used as evidence in the final assessment report that John's social worker presented at court as they showed clear progression in their relationship.

John was initially very distrustful of his mother when contact was resumed between them. He believed that she would lie to him and was only confident to take part in the sessions as he trusted his foster carer. However, once the life story work began and they started to talk to each other about their shared history, their relationship began to improve. For the first time, John was able to ask questions of someone in his family and to be given accurate information relating to his life. This information was not always easy to hear, especially in relation to his mother and father's relationship (which had been very violent at times) but Stacey did her best to give him the details without apportioning blame, and she was willing to admit her own shortcomings and to apologise for the times she did not put his needs first. This was significant for both Stacey and John as it gave them an opportunity to begin a new relationship that was based on openness and honesty and a clear attachment began to develop between them.

This work allowed John the opportunity to discuss the story that he had been given by his grandparents and for his mother to offer an alternative reality, in which she had not abandoned him and had never given up on him or forgotten him. John wanted proof that what his mother was saying was true, as he had very few memories of her being in his life at all, and she was able to show him pictures of their time together. She had kept photographs of birthday parties, Christmas contact sessions, days out, as well as the places in which they had lived, his first day at nursery, and dozens of him as a baby and toddler whilst he was living with her.

Stacey had also kept his identity bracelet from hospital when he was born, cards and calendars he had made at school or nursery, paintings he had made during contact sessions and even the pyjamas he had been wearing when she rescued him from the fire. John felt that this was a clear demonstration of his mother continuing to care for him even when she was prevented from seeing him, and that she had always loved him.

The story that Stacey shared with John was that he had lived with paternal grandparents for almost eight years; he had been placed with them by his mother following the house fire in which they both almost died. John was only four at the time and his mother had broken a bedroom window and lowered him out of it and dropped him onto bedding she had thrown down. She then lowered herself from the window and dropped into the garden next to him, saving them both. This fire left them homeless and Stacey felt she was left with little option but to place John with members of their own family rather than allow Children's Services to put him in a foster placement. His grandparents applied for a residence order shortly afterwards, which John's mother agreed to at the time, mistakenly believing that this was a temporary solution. Children's Services ceased to have any involvement with the family when the order was granted.

John had regular contact with his mother until 2010, when it ended abruptly; he was led to believe that his mother no longer wanted to see him and he was very angry and hurt by her rejection of him. After contact with his mother came to an end, John's behaviour at school and home deteriorated rapidly, and he was eventually transferred to a special school for children with emotional and behavioural difficulties. Stacey was by this time living in her own flat with a new partner and she petitioned the court for contact with her son to be resumed.

As John got older, his grandparents struggled to cope with his behaviour as he had regular angry and sometimes violent outbursts; he became very withdrawn and retreated to his bedroom, where he played day and night on his XBox, only leaving when he was foraging for food, often during the night, and on the occasions he decided to go to school. When he was eventually removed from his grandparents' care by the police, he believed that it would only be for a short period and he would probably be returned to them quickly. He continued to have contact with them and his dad for the first few months he lived in foster care; however, they chose to suspend contact once he started to see his mother again regularly, telling him he had to "choose" between them.

It became clear throughout the sessions that Stacey was benefiting from the work almost as much as John was. She was able to share her own history of being "in care" with him and they both developed a deeper understanding of what had happened to each of them throughout their lives. Stacey began to see how her own experience of being parented had not been particularly positive and how this had influenced her own parenting ability and, in particular, her view of social workers and their roles within her and her child's life. She began to accept help from them and opened up about not only her concerns about the past but her wishes and dreams for the future as well. Stacey initially relied heavily on John's foster carer for support and asked for advice on how to deal with situations that arose as a result of John feeling more confident to ask his mother questions about his life. However, as the sessions progressed and the contact between the two was increased, it became obvious that Stacey had begun to develop a belief in her own abilities as a parent and felt able to deal with more and more issues on her own. This, in turn, allowed John to feel more confident that his mother was in control and that she would be able to deal with issues as they arose.

The photographs and some of the other evidence relating to John's early life that had been collected throughout the sessions were collated into an album and some narrative of the events they depicted was added by the foster carer. On the day that John left the placement and was returned to the care of his mother, the album was given to him and both John and Stacey were delighted with the result. A comprehensive record of John's life: in short, a life story book.

In order for John and his mother to be able to move on into the future together, it was imperative that they addressed the past and developed a shared understanding of their history. The successful conclusion of this piece of work was instrumental in ensuring that the rehabilitation plan for John was a positive experience and that the chances of it succeeding were increased dramatically.

Conclusion

During the time when John was separated from his mother, his sense of self-worth had suffered because he had come to believe that first his mother and then his father had rejected him. Naturally his behaviour had become difficult due to his anger about his situation and even an experienced carer found him challenging. His prospects in care were not good.

His mother had not abandoned or rejected him and had never given up hope of having him back. However, simply returning him to his mother without resolving these two different views of the past would have put great strain on them both and it is possible that their relationship would not have survived and John would have returned to care with yet another perceived rejection.

Doing life story work with John and his mother was a way of resolving these different views and restoring some of his sense of worth when he found his mother had kept all the keepsakes for him and had not rejected him. This put him in a far better position to handle the return to his mother's care and he is coping quite well with the transition.

Similarly John's mother was able to restore some of her sense of worth by having the opportunity to tell her story and show that she had kept faith with John while he was separated from her. She was in a better position to see what made John tick and what his feelings about her were.

Life story work has many uses but one of the most important is to recover the past and provide an opportunity to explain and understand what really happened, especially in situations where demonisation of parents or children has affected relationships and where the past needs to be demystified before they can move on and face new challenges.

16 Life story work in other settings

There are many different circumstances in which life story work can be used to facilitate communication and help children, and adults, through painful periods of their lives. Maureen Hitcham, Jean Lovie and Gerrilyn Smith describe three different contexts in which life story work has proved effective.

At the time of writing, Maureen Hitcham was a paediatric oncology social worker in Newcastle.

Life story work with children suffering a life-threatening illness

Maureen Hitcham

The diagnosis of childhood cancer is an unwanted, unexpected and devastating discovery. Although the outlook for most newly-diagnosed children is optimistic, there can be no guarantees of a cure. The sad reality is that many will suffer some form of emotional disturbance and/or physical or learning disability. Some will bravely struggle with the illness and its treatment but die.

Life story books and video diaries can help such children and their families cope with the intense feelings and emotions aroused when living with the strain and uncertainty of a life-threatening condition.

Stephen's story

I met Stephen on my first day as a Malcolm Sargent social worker. He was a bright, mischievous four-year-old with a lively personality and good sense of humour; he also had cancer. My plans for him included a life story book. One month after we met, I drove Stephen to his parents' home with the news that he had only days to live. I had sensed and been on the receiving end of his frustration and anger, much of which was directed at the intravenous drip administering the chemotherapy that made him feel so sick. We managed only two small pieces of work – the first was the planned use of drawings to acknowledge and deal with Stephen's anger.

Stephen

I don't like
you drip
I would like to punch you
because you make me feel sick

*In this drawing,
Stephen compares
the facial expressions
before and after
dealing with his anger*

He scribbled fiercely over some of the drawings saying how much he hated the drip.

The second piece of work was my spontaneous response to hearing he had only days to live. It was mid-December and he was going home to celebrate the arrival of Father Christmas early. We spent the last hour before leaving the hospital making a Christmas card for his parents. Despite being very weak and very breathless, Stephen worked enthusiastically and with great excitement. There was a real sense of achievement for both of us on completion. I know now that this was also my way of saying sorry to his parents for all the things I had not been able to do. Stephen died on 18 December at home.

Sadly there isn't always the luxury of time to plan, when working with gravely ill children. This does not mean that we should disregard good practice, but we may have to acknowledge at the outset that many of the agreed goals may not be reached despite a willingness and determination on the part of both child and worker. Workers may subsequently be left with a number of unresolved feelings. In view of the complexity and diversity of the social work task in working with these children, regular professional and managerial supervision is essential.

This is an emotional area of work and it is normal and proper to respond emotionally. The techniques I describe here all evoke strong emotional responses; so self-awareness and an understanding of the implications for the child are essential before embarking on this work. There also needs to be an awareness of personal feelings regarding death not only as an abstract notion but also more importantly, perhaps, as a personal reality.

These techniques can all be adapted to suit you as an individual and the child with whom you are working.

Studies have shown that children who have cancer are more anxious than other children. Many of them keep their thoughts and feelings to themselves for a variety of reasons. It is important that they understand what is happening and why, so that they are able to distinguish reality from fantasy.

Graeme's story

Graeme is seven years old and suffers from Aplastic Anaemia. Although not a malignant disease, its treatment and implications are similar to cancer. As part of his treatment, Graeme had to undergo a bone marrow transplant, which is a major and hazardous procedure. Patients undergoing transplantation are at risk of infection and therefore are nursed in a sterile environment. All staff and visitors must wear gowns and masks and observe strict rules of hygiene.

The period of isolation, limitations on normal activity, restrictions on diet and free movement inevitably took their toll on Graeme. Not surprisingly he could be surly, aggressive and very demanding. No one felt sure how Graeme was feeling or what his understanding of the illness and treatment was.

Graeme did not easily share thoughts and feelings and was not well enough or interested enough to undertake traditional life story work. But

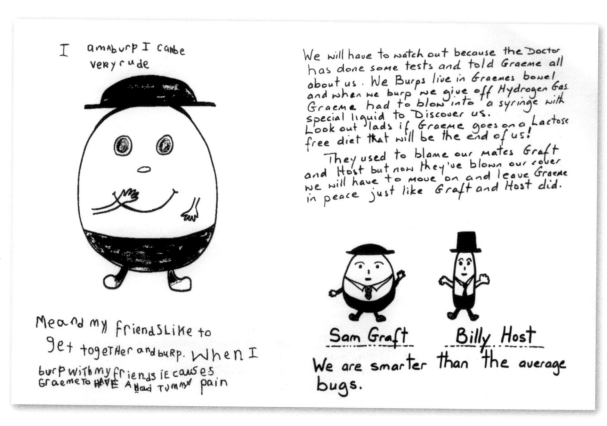

Illustration by Graeme

in his case, producing a video diary seemed to have provided him with a non-threatening and enjoyable opportunity to sort out and know the facts about his illness and its treatment, which hopefully left him feeling less at the mercy of uncontrollable events.

He was in fact the first child with whom I used a video camera and his response was remarkable. On film, he freely shares his thoughts, feelings and understanding of his condition and its treatment. He describes how there is a war going on inside his body called the SS War: SS meaning Saddam and Smith (his surname). Saddam represents the bad cells, Smith the good cells. He humorously and imaginatively describes the chemotherapy bombing Saddam in order to make room for the good cells to grow. When asked who he thought would win the war he replied, 'Well, at first I thought it would be Saddam but now I think it will be Smith!' Graeme proudly showed his family and staff this short video and later went on to record further footage discussing the profound effect the illness has had on his nine-year-old sister Rachel.

More recently Graeme has received treatment for a condition known as Graft versus Host Disease. This caused him to suffer repeated unpleasant physical experiences mainly in the form of severe abdominal pain. Graeme became depressed and irritable and withdrew from everyday activities. Tests showed his Graft Versus Host Disease was improving and that his discomfort was the result of lactose intolerance. There were two main ways to reduce Graeme's distress. One was to increase his pain control, the other was to reduce his emotional stress by giving him adequate explanations of his experiences so that he was able to make sense of what was going on and begin to anticipate the future without despair. I engaged him in the piece of work below that will be incorporated into his video diary.

The change in his personality whilst producing this work was quite remarkable. Apathy and irritability were quickly replaced with energy, enthusiasm and excitement.

Working with siblings

When children receive their first diagnosis, they are confronted with many new experiences. It may be their first hospitalisation, when they are subjected to painful tests and they have to develop trust in the changing hospital staff. They see and sense the anxiety of their families and suddenly their lives are out of their control and they are scared. It is therefore not surprising that as friends, relatives, neighbours and parents, all our concern and attention is focused on the sick child. But what about the siblings?

The healthy siblings of children with a chronic life-threatening illness face many sources of distress. There is the initial turmoil of diagnosis, separation from loved ones during treatment, and the absolute chaos and unpredictability leaving them bereft of normal family life. Their parents often lack the energy to identify or respond to the emotional needs of anyone other than the sick child. This can create overwhelming feelings of anger, jealousy, sadness and fear. Intervention with all family members is vital if we are to combat such potentially damaging feelings and create a safe, non-threatening environment in which they can begin to share and explore these thoughts and experiences. In the school setting, brothers and sisters are having to mix with peers whose lives have a completely different agenda.

Life story books have proved very successful in helping these children understand their worlds and where they fit in relation to the family, the illness, the hospital and medical personnel. Art and imagery often provide an initial form of communication for those children who won't or can't talk about their feelings. These feelings are recorded, visually unexpressed, but then safely retained in a life story book to be used over and over again once they are ready – verbal communication often follows very quickly and with surprising fluency as some of these examples show.

Using life story work with families affected by HIV

Jean Lovie

At the time of writing, Jean Lovie was an HIV/AIDS Services Development Officer, Newcastle City Council.

The death of a parent or close family member presents a child with a very particular challenge. With HIV infection, death is likely to occur after months, possibly years, of intermittent but progressively serious illness which disrupts family life. There may be more than one family member ill or dying, often cloaked in secrecy thereby increasing the child's loneliness.

Patients ill with HIV infection are frequently profoundly fatigued. They are likely to be younger parents trying to come to terms with their own anger and sadness. They may intend to help a child prepare for change but sometimes these plans can be almost too painful or hard to implement.

Ways of helping children have to be found that are:

- flexible
- pleasurable
- relatively easy to use
- of value to all ages, including children with no or limited reading skills
- adaptable to fast-changing events.

Life story work using family photographs has proved to be one useful method with some families.

Kate and Ben's story

Kate was four, Ben, her brother, two. Their father had been diagnosed HIV-infected before they were born but their mother, Kate and Ben were non-infected. Kate's playgroup leader, the health visitor and the childminder knew of their father's HIV positive status, as the parents had decided that they would be better able to understand the pressures placed upon the family if they were in the picture. The family was also in regular contact with a hospital social worker.

Four weeks before her father's death, Kate began waking up at night screaming. She knew her father was very ill – time had been taken to answer the questions she had asked. She was unable to say why she was frightened or what exactly was wrong. She wanted to visit her father in hospital and to continue bringing the drawings she had done in playgroup, but she asked to visit less frequently. Her explanation was that the nurses would look after him now. She appeared clearly aware of what was happening but unsure how to express what she thought or was feeling. A way had to be found of helping her to do this.

A known and trusted aunt came to stay. Her mother was able to spend more time at the hospital and Kate was given time and space for herself. On a daily basis, at Kate's pace, family photographs were collected and placed chronologically in a book. Her parents' lives were plotted out, recording an event, the year it happened and, if appropriate, Kate's age at the time. Kate's own photographs were added and those of Ben, her grandparents and close aunts and uncles. The starting point was her parents' birth, then their schooling, hobbies, courtship, marriage, her father's illness, and her own and Ben's birth. To this were added fun experiences they had shared as a family.

As the strength of the family system around her became clearer, Kate chose to say she knew her father was dying. As the work progressed, her nightmares receded. Care was taken to answer her questions honestly, including the input of various family members into her life. The book was completed in outline by the time of her father's death. Other close family members brought photographs for the book to the funeral.

Since then Kate's mother has remarried. Her stepfather has learned about Kate's father from the book, and his photograph has also been added. Major family events subsequent to her father's death have been included. Kate still reads the book when she is upset or worried, leaving it out for her mother to see as a signal that she wants help. It has come to be used less as she has adapted to her new life.

The successful outcome in this case depended on:

- the availability of a trusted and close family member who knew everyone in the family and was able to separate out her own feelings and those of Kate about what was happening;

- the availability of an outside facilitator – in this instance a social worker – with whom the interpretation of the ongoing work could be shared;

- the availability of photographs over a period of time;

- an understanding of the family's circumstances. The life story work was part of the help offered to the family in a number of ways. The timing of the life story work in relation to events at the hospital was crucial.

Kate used the photographs to express her awareness of her father's changing appearance in the months before his death as he had become more unwell; she was then able to say she realised he would not return home. Through the photographs, the size and strengths of the family network were conveyed.

This approach has been used in similar circumstances with another child of about the same age. In both instances the children were willing to co-operate for a limited time and had, before the work, considerable self-awareness. While life story work may not be appropriate for all families in these circumstances, it has already proved valuable for some.

Life story work with adults

Gerrilyn Smith

Adults, too, can benefit from making a record of their own early lives, or those of their children. This is especially important for those adults who themselves grew up in the care system. Going back to the places of their childhood can be very therapeutic and help them put their current lives into perspective.

There will be many adults who grew up "in care" who will not have had the benefit of someone taking the time to chart with them their lives and moves through the care system. Gaining access to social service files is one way of trying to piece together their past.

The following is an example of some life story work with an adult who was herself in care.

VANESSA'S STORY

Vanessa was 24 when she was referred to me. She had three children under five years, and had recently had a stillbirth. She wasn't coping with the children and they were removed from her care while she tried to sort herself out. (This was prior to the Adoption and Children Act 2002.) Among the list of things we agreed to work on, Vanessa expressed an interest in doing a life story book for herself. This was currently being done with her children and I felt it might help her understand what was happening for them.

We started with a family tree, going back to Vanessa's grandparents. Vanessa knew her paternal grandparents; however, she possessed no information about her maternal grandparents. Vanessa was of dual heritage – her mother was Spanish and her father from an island in the Caribbean. She began her life story book with the following introduction:

This diary is to help me and others understand the difficulty of life in being a single parent and having to bring children up on your own. It also tells you about the life I had and why I am the way I am now.

She began to write of her earliest memories starting with recollections of her life in a convent and of occasional visits from her mother. The first chapter ends at her fifth birthday when she is supposed to return to live with her mother. The second chapter begins with Vanessa's paternal grandmother coming to take her to live with her. Whilst living with her granny, Vanessa had more contact with her father.

Vanessa continued writing another 28 chapters of her life. We went over them together talking about her memories, sorting out some confusion and thinking about how her own childhood affected her capacity to parent.

We were able to identify patterns in her life that were being repeated with her children. Vanessa's own mother wouldn't help us with Vanessa's life story book. We wrote to her and went round to visit her, but she refused to participate. Her mother's partner wouldn't let Vanessa speak to her. In reviewing her childhood, Vanessa was able to see that her parents' partners (they were no longer together) frequently stopped Vanessa and her siblings from getting closer to their birth parents. Vanessa was in her third relationship but felt that, unlike her parents' partners, her current partner was able to view Vanessa's children as his own.

We made a list of places she wanted to visit for her life story book. We collected together important mementos she wanted to keep. These included her children's health record books, the important Christmas and birthday cards, photographs of the children from the residential units they were currently in, and photographs from our round of visits.

We started with a visit to her paternal grandmother's house. We went to several residential units where Vanessa had lived. Many were still being used as homes but not necessarily for young people. In one case the building had been knocked down and only a pile of rubble remained. We visited Vanessa's old secondary school and, with permission, walked around.

It was also important to begin collecting mementos for her children. We went to the hospitals where her children were born, houses and flats where she had previously lived, the nursery the children had attended. Vanessa began to make scrapbooks for her children. She began preparing for them to not move on to foster families, but to return to her and start again.

Whilst the children did spend a period of time away from her, she continued to be involved in their care. She visited regularly and predictably. She tried hard to stay connected to her children in a way that her parents had not stayed connected to her. She reflected on her network of friends, many of whom were younger and didn't have the responsibility of looking after children, and who were not encouraging her to keep up contact. She started to meet other young mothers. She began to identify what needed to change before she felt able to resume care of her children. Whilst the life story book was not the only piece of work done with her, it provided a useful focus. It helped her recognise unhelpful patterns in her own childhood – patterns she was determined not to repeat.

Part of what helped Vanessa was someone taking an interest in her childhood. It is very difficult for many parents who experience difficulty in parenting to allow their children to benefit from experiences that they themselves were not offered or were deprived of. By doing Vanessa's life story book, I was able to point out how well she had already done and how she had begun to make changes in the family patterns. Although Vanessa was still very angry with her mother, she had a greater understanding of the difficulties she must have experienced. Vanessa also felt able to reconnect with her father and to ask him for more information about their family.

Unlike other types of individual work with adults, which often occurs in the counsellor's office, Vanessa and I talked in the car on our journeys, in cafes, and in the places that were important to her. The tangible reminders of her past also meant she remembered more and was able to recount in greater detail aspects of her childhood that she had not thought about in a long time. In doing so, we arrived at a better understanding of why Vanessa was the way she was, and began the process of getting her to think about how she would like to be, as a woman, as a partner and as a mother.

17 Life story work with teenagers who have made contact with their birth parents via social media

Sarah Ryan

Sarah Ryan qualified as a social worker in 1990 with an MSW from York University and since 2004 has worked in the adoption support team in Leeds City Council. She has always believed in life story work as an effective way of helping children make sense of their early life history, their journey and their inner self.

Contact through social media

In 2009/2010, I and my colleagues began receiving referrals about adopted children who had made contact with their birth relatives on Facebook. We were being approached by birth family members and adoptive parents, both of whom felt unprepared to handle this unexpected contact and wanted help and guidance on managing it. For birth family members, such contact can trigger strong emotions about unresolved issues that they don't feel able to deal with; for adoptive parents, the fact of their child making contact with their birth family in this way is frightening and destabilising. During this time, we were responding to these family "crises" of unplanned, unregulated and unmanageable contact with none of the parties being prepared for the impact it was having.

Generally, the contact appears to be initiated by the adopted young person, but there are also situations in which birth relatives have managed to identify their birth child and initiate contact. Although the latter scenario is much less common, its impact is huge and can be especially traumatising as it can threaten the adopted child's sense of safety.

Any kind of communication via social media is immediate. Contact made via Facebook is instantaneous and will most likely be on a device – computer, tablet or phone – to which the young person will have immediate, and probably sole, access. Such contact does not allow for any exploration of what might be going on for whichever family is approached and then becomes involved. In cases where children have been removed from unsafe, harmful birth families, and have then unexpectedly been contacted by them, it can shatter their sense of safety and retrigger childhood experiences; it can also question the ability of their adoptive parent to keep them safe. This can be devastating for adoptive families who have worked hard to give their children a sense of security.

When such contact is made with adopted adolescents, it can hardly come at a worse time, as teenagers go through massive physical, cognitive and social changes in this period. Adolescence is a difficult stage for all young people and being adopted adds a further layer of complexity. This is a time when teenagers are trying to separate from their parents but adopted teenagers are also grappling with their identity: Who am I? Where do I belong? What about my birth family? Where are they now? Do I have brothers or sisters? It can become an all-consuming preoccupation and be a very confusing time.

If adopted teenagers are thinking about their birth family and curious about them, making contact via social media is easy, accessible and tempting. Some adolescents, especially those who have experienced neglect and trauma in their early lives, have limited "cause and effect" thinking, are impulsive and are vulnerable to risk, and it is precisely at this stage in their development that they are less likely to enlist the guidance and support of their parents or other adults. Facebook is not actually the cause of the problem but its features – the ability to search for and find people, and the ease with which you can message them – have contributed to creating a means of making contact that is impulsive, spontaneous, unmanaged, and sometimes unsafe. Two books, one aimed at social workers, the other at adoptive parents, give information on managing social media and contact within adoption – *Social Networking and Contact*, and *Facing up to Facebook* (Fursland, 2010, 2013).

How can life story work help?

If an adopted young person does not have a working knowledge or a coherent script of their birth history, including why they needed to be removed from the care of their birth parents, they can be open to accepting a different version of events. In cases where unmediated contact has suddenly taken place with birth parents, it can be all too easy to believe the latter's account of what happened. Crucially, at the very point of contact being made, the opportunity to work with the young person, independent of this influence and the complications of this new relationship, is compromised or lost. Worse still, it can place a barrier between the adoptive parent and their teenager, making it harder for the former to help support their child to navigate a challenging situation at a time when they need it most.

For adopted young people, the desire to find out about their origins is natural and they may have questions about their past and their heritage that their adoptive parents cannot answer. In such cases, it will be inevitable that their curiosity will deepen and the urge to even meet their birth family will be strong. What role can life story work play in such situations? Below I describe some work I did with Beth (name changed) to illustrate how life story work can help.

Working with Beth and her family

Beth's adoptive parents had been receiving irregular letterbox contact from her birth family but had not received any letters for two years. Beth knew her birth parents were still together and had gone on to have three more children who lived with them at home.

Beth had been removed due to non-accidental injuries found on her older half-siblings. Social services believed her birth father could have been responsible, and as a result of his refusal to take part in a residential parent and baby assessment or leave the family home, Beth was placed for adoption.

At the age of 14, Beth found her birth sister, Ruby, who is 15 months younger than her, on Facebook; she knew her sister's first name as well as her birth surname. She also made contact with her birth mother. They all exchanged mobile numbers immediately. By the time Beth's adoptive parents knew that contact had been established, there had been numerous phone calls, texts, exchanges on Facebook and even visits to the birth family home.

The first meeting

In situations like these, it is necessary to embark on intensive life story work and to do so quickly. I generally commit to weekly meetings and make some time to learn a bit about the young person from their parents. Parents are invited to be part of all or some of the work and helped to decide this with their son/daughter.

Unlike life story work in other settings, in which you have more time to build up a working relationship with the young person, teenagers may resist engaging in this way. So to get them to engage, I invite them to formulate questions they may have wanted to ask about their adoption even before they made contact with their birth family. Often adopted young people can't imagine that anyone might understand their feelings about being adopted or their curiosity and longing to know about their birth family. They may not be able to put this into words and it is helpful to acknowledge this with them. So in my work with Beth, I shared with her a worksheet that shows some of the things that other adopted young people have told me. (My inspiration for this came from reading *Twenty Things Adopted Kids Wish their Adoptive Parents Knew*, by Sherrie Eldridge, 1999.)

Things young adopted people feel

The worksheet gives the message at the very outset that you know that the young person will have questions and thoughts and mixed feelings about their birth family, and that this is OK and this is what the life story work will be about.

I wanted Beth to know that, although she had initiated the contact, if it was proving too confusing and/or overwhelming for her on her own, we could manage it together; if she wanted, we could slow it down. Beth's mum explained to her that I was there to help them to think about what she might want to happen with contact with her birth family and that she wanted to be there to support her.

It was important to let Beth know that I was not trying to stop all contact but just give her an opportunity to pause and think about it and to help her prepare for it so that it was manageable and she was safe. With her mum's help, Beth was able to tell me with whom she had had contact in her birth family. At this point, I did not go into the why and how, and just accepted that she had acted on her curiosity.

In the first meeting, I also let Beth know that I had access to her birth records and could help her answer some questions about how she came to be adopted. I made sure I had read the Form E, knew the circumstances of her adoption, and was aware of the issues that might emerge. I acknowledged that her birth parents staying together and going on to have three more children was a difficult situation for any adopted young person to accept and that I knew that she must have strong feelings about what had happened. Understandably, Beth had questions about why she had been adopted and they had not. She had also now met her brothers and sisters and wanted to have relationships with them, but the contact between Beth and Ruby had already become disruptive, and they were both already managing difficulties with boyfriends and friends, and also at school, and Beth was self-harming. Additionally, neither Beth nor Ruby were able to manage the contact they had with each other on social media: they did not have boundaries and became intensely competitive and hostile.

It was important that Beth knew that she would be part of any decision-making about the contact, along with her adoptive parents. I told her that although we wouldn't be stopping contact completely, we would be slowing it down so that everyone knew what they could expect and work out what was right for them. (I had agreed this with Beth's parents first.) It was important that Beth had a means of contributing to the plans, and life story work was a means for her to explore this.

I explained to Beth that there was legislation about contact for adopted people and that her parents would need to support her and give consent to the contact. It can be reassuring and helpful for some teenagers to know that there is a legal framework that holds contact in place; this can help them not feel so individually responsible for contact that has already become overwhelming or beyond their capacity to manage on their own.

We made a spider graph of what was going on for Beth in her life.

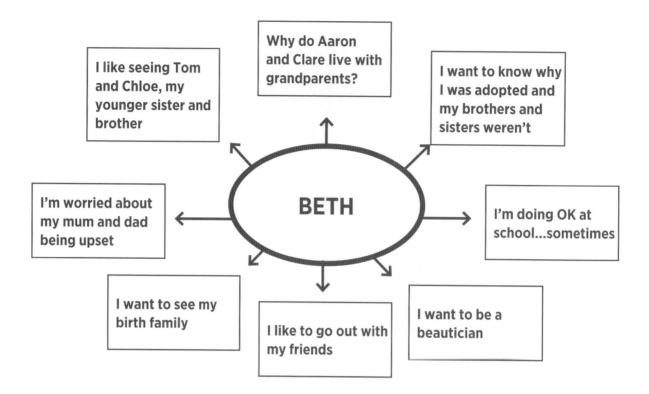

From this I learnt a bit more about Beth and we identified some of her questions about her own adoption and agreed that, in the next session, we would construct a timeline of how the decisions had been made for her to be adopted.

Subsequent sessions

Initially, life story work with Beth focused around her early life and how and why certain decisions had been made by social services. We considered the criteria that would have led to this decision and been significant at that time, and identified that keeping babies safe was the paramount reason for why she had been removed. It was important that Beth be given the opportunity to explore the strengths and risks in her birth family at the time that the decision had been made for her to be adopted so that she could compare those with the strengths and risks in the present day and see if anything had changed. This involved an exploration of the risks to children and the responsibility of parents to keep their children safe. We revisited the reason for her having been adopted – injuries to older siblings that her birth father and birth mother had not been able to explain (her older siblings had been placed with their maternal grandparents and still lived with them). This work helped Beth to have a narrative to compare to the version of events she was being given by her birth parents.

The other part of the life story work was about making sense of the here and now, both in her birth family and at home with her adoptive parents. We used spider graphs, sculpting and pie charts to map this out. Older children can work with these as a way of visualising what is going on for them, to help organise their thinking, and identify the different parts of themselves.

Below is an example of one of the spider graphs we drew in our sessions. During this time, contact by text and Facebook was ongoing and face-to-face contact had been limited, structured and planned.

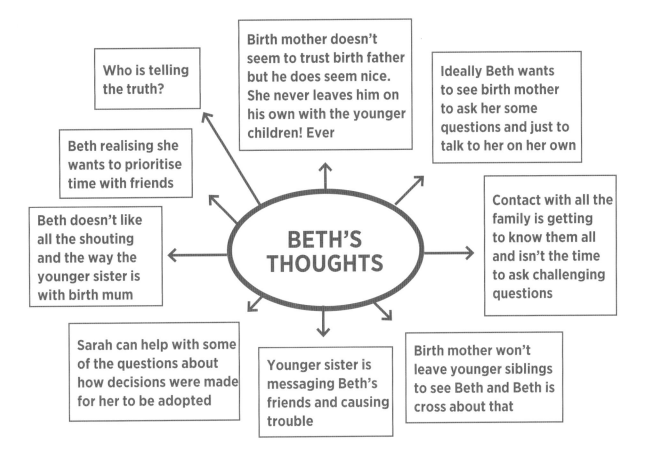

In another session, we used gemstones and made a sculpt of all the people Beth was thinking about and what she was feeling towards them.

Throughout these sessions we were able to explore the themes that were important to Beth:

- her feelings of rejection that her birth mother would not make time for her above and without her siblings;

- her observations about her birth parents' ongoing volatile relationship;

- how her birth mother, after all these years, still didn't trust her birth father alone with the younger children.

Beth really liked having a little brother and sister and seeing them was a strong pull. We spent time thinking about how she felt about her younger sister and why that might be. Her sister had been born 15 months after Beth and this time her parents had agreed to the residential assessment and were able to keep her. It was clear that both sisters were vulnerable and involved in some harmful and risk-taking behaviours. They felt competitive and with access to each others' Facebook friends, it was hard to contain the damage they did to each other by becoming involved with each other's friends.

Doing the life story work gave Beth some factual information about the decisions made for and about her and helped to place this within a timescale. This didn't stop Beth from feeling sad, but the work gave her an opportunity to be heard and to express her feelings about being adopted and helped her to process them. Doing the sessions with her adoptive parents helped them maintain a connection at a volatile time and share each others' feelings.

In preparation for this, I had devised a "feelings" worksheet.

Feelings I have when I think about my birth family

Scared		Pleased		Angry
Cautious	Excited		Curious	
Nervous		Terrified		Dumb
Numb	Impatient		Overwhelmed	
(Anxious)		Emotional		Tearful
(Left out)	Hopeful		Confused	
Threatened		Protective		(Loyal)
Disloyal	Speechless		Sad	
Small		Guilty		Rushed
Out of control	Unsure		Vulnerable	
Responsible		Worried		Hesitant
Weird	Shocked		Disappointed	
Embarrassed		(At last)		Can't wait

I gave both Beth and her mother the same worksheet and different coloured pens. I asked them separately to circle the emotion they each thought Beth might have towards her birth mother (you can substitute this with different relatives as appropriate). They then read them out to each other. This helped them to share and communicate their feelings, and opened up discussions between them about what other feelings Beth may have. I then got them to do the exercise again, but this time about what Beth's mother might be feeling about Beth's contact with her birth mum. Young people in this situation often don't think that their contact with their birth family will have any impact on their adoptive parents and need help to be aware of this.

Finally, they did a third exercise, both of them separately identifying the feelings they thought that Beth's birth mum or other relatives might have about the contact. This is not always appropriate or possible to do at an early stage and is more useful when a future contact is being planned. This was helpful for Beth as she was constantly barraging her birth mum with demands to meet, while the latter struggled to make herself available for Beth. Obviously the life story work exposed the difficulties that Beth was having in managing the realisation that her birth mother couldn't give her the level of contact she was asking for. This resulted in us putting therapeutic support in place for Beth.

Contact with the birth family through social media can severely test relationships in the adoptive family and doing life story work with the young person and their adoptive parents can strengthen their relationship. It gives adoptive parents an opportunity to see their child not as a teenager who is rejecting them in favour of their birth family, but as a child who is confused, grieving and in need of emotional support.

Together with Beth's adoptive mum, we created a spider graph about the things Beth liked about being in her family. Beth's parents were able to recognise that they could create opportunities to reinforce their love and need to care for her. So they returned to spending time with her in ways they hadn't done for a while – film and popcorn nights, shopping and other activities, and pampered her, thus demonstrating to Beth that they were emotionally available to her. It helped reinforce Beth's feelings of safety in the family, especially as her feelings of rejection by her birth family grew.

> 'As parent and child construct and reconstruct stories of their experiences together, perspectives can be dramatically changed and relationships healed.' Golding and Hughes (2012)

Other learning

Adoptive parents feel destabilised by their child's contact with birth parents and need support to think about their fears and worries, the shift in their relationship, and any loss of confidence in their parenting. They also need to have an understanding of what is going on for their adopted child in needing to resolve identity issues and gain a sense of who they are. **Birth parents** too need the opportunity to talk about their experiences of the adoption and of being contacted by social media and be given support to manage it. When contact with the immediate birth family is difficult, there may be other birth relatives, like an aunt or grandparent, who could help in providing additional information on the young person's story.

The **life story work** highlighted that Beth needed further therapeutic help and that life story work in itself would not help resolve her problems; workers need to be aware of their responsibility in engaging the family with other support services where needed.

Early life story work – a protective factor

In my work with adolescents (and their families) already engaged in some contact with their birth families, it has become clear that they would have been better prepared for the impact of contact if they had been able to process their early history at an earlier developmental stage rather than at adolescence. I have seen that for older adopted children, the direct contact with their birth family could trigger a whole range of responses including psychological stress, emotional unbalance and behavioural difficulties. Adopted children cannot understand these triggers unless they have had the opportunity to explore their own early history.

Adoptive parents have a hard task of knowing when or how to share difficult information, waiting until they feel their child is mature enough to manage it. However, it is important that adopted children grow up within an openness and a rich life story to satisfy their curiosity and avoid fantasies and idealisation. Delaying sharing information can also be a problem; adolescence is not the best time for parents to share information they may have withheld (with every good intention), as teenagers are more likely to react emotionally or feel they cannot trust their parents to be honest with them. Early life story work with children between 7 and 11 years can be a protective factor when considering and managing future contact with birth parents.

18 After life story work

Later life letters

Later life letters are not new; providing them has been part of good adoption practice in the UK for over 30 years, and making them a requirement of the Adoption Agencies Regulations serves to accentuate their importance as an important addition to life story work.

A later life letter is now required under Schedule 5, The Adoption Agencies Regulations 2005 (England and Wales). Paragraph 8 mentions 'the dates on which the child's life story book and later life letter are to be passed by the adoption agency to the prospective adopters'. Although not a requirement of legislation elsewhere in the UK, it is nevertheless considered to be good practice, and should be applied to children who are in long-term foster care or placed with friends and families.

A later life letter is an opportunity to explain in a letter the events in the child's life up to the point of being adopted. This opportunity should be grasped to explain these events in enough detail to enable the child to have an understanding as to why he or she can no longer live with their family of origin. Providing the facts about a child's family of origin will help dispel any fantasies he or she may have about it and the reality will help dispel negative ideas such as 'I am to blame for what happened'. Reaching an understanding as to how this came about may be a long process and the later life letter is another means of facilitating this process. A good practice guide entitled *Writing a Later Life Letter* (Moffat, 2012) provides practical information on what should and should not be included in a later life letter, how to explain difficult or painful issues, and the place of the letter within life story work; it also contains useful examples.

How should the letter be written?

The guidance to the Adoption and Children Act 2002 suggests that the contents 'should be in sufficient detail so that in the future the adolescent child or young adult will know about his or her natural family'. Some adoption workers suggest that, as well as a later life letter for the young adult, another letter should be written for the pre-adolescent child. Whilst this would be useful, we wonder how realistic this would be, given time constraints.

The following is a suggested structure for the later life letter; overall, we believe that its parameters should be determined by the known facts, with some explanation of why things happened e.g. why an Emergency Protection Order was made; it is important not to make assumptions because at a later date these could be shown to be incorrect.

The guidance to the Adoption and Children Act 2002 proposes that the 'child's natural family could be asked to write either their own letters to the child or contributions for the agency's letter if the agency considers either of these methods appropriate'. We consider this is an excellent suggestion provided that help and support are given to the birth family to accomplish this. These letters can be hugely meaningful for children later on and should be safely scanned, stored and kept in the child's records.

We use the following headings as a framework, which we "mix and match".

Reason for writing the letter

I write this letter with the knowledge that your parents will have, over the years, explained how you came to live with and be adopted by them.

Information about their birth

You were born on .... at St James' Hospital, Leeds, and weighed ....

Information about birth parents

Your birth mother is Gillian Roberts. She was 18 years old at the time of your birth and her date of birth is ....

(Include details of personality, physical appearance, employment, etc. Brief details of birth family.)

Birth father

Similar details as for birth mother. If his identity is not known, include details that have been ascertained and from what source.

Details of birth parent's relationship

Whether they were married to each other, lived together, divorced

....

Include particulars of children they had within this relationship (full siblings) and their whereabouts. Also include particulars of children they had within previous and subsequent relationships (half-siblings) and their whereabouts. Make reference to their family tree in their life story book.

In our experience, in later life, a person who was adopted feels a sense of anguish and loss about the siblings from whom they became separated through adoption.

Explanation of why they became adopted

This is the difficult part of the letter because the temptation is to include much of the considerable detail that will be contained in the various reports that will have been written already by this stage. It is prudent to resist this temptation to include explicit detail, some of which is best imparted through counselling when an adopted person requests access to their birth records. The purpose here is to provide an understanding of events that happened up to the point of either adoption or other permanent care. Nonetheless, the complexity of a child's background inevitably leads to a letter of several pages. Vera Falhberg, who considers that the task is one of helping the person understand the reality and not protecting them from it, provides useful guidance. Already there will be a chronology completed and this will be a useful starting point as will the life graph in their life story book.

We find it helpful to include information about the birth parent's own childhood, particularly if this was a contributory factor in their inability to parent adequately. Next we include information of events that led to the child being removed from his or her birth family. Here comes the difficult part, for example, if the child was sexually abused – how can this be explained in the letter? Remember, the adopted person will not be reading the letter in isolation; the letter will have been passed to him or her through their adoptive parents who should be aware of the issues that will arise. It is important not to sanitise events, which can lead to misunderstanding, especially when there will have been clear reasons why the child was removed from his or her family of origin. It is vital to provide reliable information about birth families if keeping the adopted person safe in later life is an issue. Nonetheless, it can sometimes be appropriate not to give precise facts. We usually write along the following lines.

You were hurt by your birth mother's partner, Lee, and the doctor who examined you was so concerned that he immediately involved social workers who were experienced in child protection work. Gillian wanted to continue living with Lee and therefore if you returned to them you were in danger of being harmed again. Lee was charged by the police with hurting you and was sent to prison.

We use the life graph events as building blocks to complete the letter. Once you have drafted the letter, it is essential that its contents be discussed with a person who is skilled and experienced in this work in order that it be refined and amended appropriately.

Ending the letter

Ending the letter should leave open the opportunity to contact adoption support services for help and advice, if needed.

I hope this letter helps you understand what happened to you when you were a child and living with your birth family. In the future you may want to know more detail than is contained in this letter. At the time of my writing this, you are a delightful four-year-old, happy and content with your parents who will be there as you grow older to answer questions you may ask. When you are 18 years old, you can ask to see the social services file that contains a record of your life until you were adopted. If, before you reach this age, you want to know more, you can ask your parents to approach our adoption support service, which may be able to assist.

Keeping contact between siblings separated by adoption

Many family groups are separated by adoption for a whole range of reasons, perhaps because of complex, competing needs which means that separating the children enhances the chances of a successful adoption or, in the case of a large sibling group, because a single family able to take all the children cannot be found. Whilst some adoptive parents are able to participate in "face-to-face" contact to enable a child to grow up with a knowledge of his or her birth siblings, sometimes this is not possible or desirable. Where this is not practicable, it may be possible for a newsletter to be collated by the agency, that is facilitating the "letterbox" contact. Each sibling or adoptive parent can send in their contribution and then the collated newsletter can be sent to all the siblings and possibly the birth family.

References

Ahmad A, Betts B and Cown L (2008) 'Using interactive media in direct practice', in Luckock B and Lefevre M (eds) *Direct Work: Social work with Children and Young People in Care*, London: BAAF, pp. 169–180

Aust PH (1981) 'Using the life story book in treatment of children in placement', *Child Welfare*, 60:8, pp 535–560

Bandura A (1977) 'Self-efficacy: towards a unifying theory of behavioural change', *Psychological Review,* 84:2, pp 191–215

Barn R (1999) *Working with Black Children and Adolescents in Need*, London: BAAF

Baynes P (2008) 'Untold stories: a discussion of life story work', *Adoption & Fostering*, 32:2, pp. 43–49

Beste HM and Richardson RG (1981) 'Developing a life story book program for foster children', *Child Welfare*, 60:8, pp 529–534

Betts B and Ahmad A (2003) *My Life Story* (CD-ROM), Orkney: Information Plus

Bowlby J (1980) *Loss: Sadness and depression*, New York, NY: Basic Books

Bowlby J (1988) *A Secure Base: Parent-child attachment and healthy human development*, New York, NY: Basic Books

Byron T (2008) *Safer Children in a Digital World: The report of the Byron Review*, London: DCSF

Byron T (2010) *Do we have Safer Children in a Digital World? A review of progress since the 2008 Byron Review*, London: DCSF

Cairns K (2002) *Attachment, Trauma and Resilience: Therapeutic caring for children*, London: BAAF

Camis J (2001) *My Life and Me*, London: BAAF

Commission for Social Care Inspection (2006) *About Adoption: A children's views report*, London: Commission for Social Care Inspection

Cook-Cottone C and Beck M (2007) 'A model for life-story work: facilitating the construction of personal narrative for foster children', *Child and Adolescent Mental Health*, 12:4, pp 193–195

Cousins J (2006) *Every Child is Special: Placing disabled children for permanence*, London: BAAF

Donley K (1981) *Opening New Doors*, London: BAAF

Eldridge S (1999) *Twenty Things Adopted Kids Wish their Adoptive Parents Knew*, New York, NY: Random House

Ellis A and Greiger R (1977) *Handbook of Rational Emotive Therapy*, New York, NY: Springer

Fahlberg V (1994) *A Child's Journey through Placement*, London: BAAF

Fivush R, Reese E and Haden CA (2006) 'Elaborating on elaborations: role of maternal reminiscing style in cognitive and socio-emotional development', *Child Development*, 77:6, pp 1568–1588

Fivush R and Vasudeva A (2002) 'Remembering to relate: socioemotional correlates of mother-child reminiscing', *Journal of Cognition and Development*, 3:1, pp 73–90

Fursland E (2010) *Social Networking and Contact: How social workers can help adoptive families*, London: BAAF

Fursland E (2013) *Facing up to Facebook: A survival guide for adoptive families*, London: BAAF

Golding KS and Hughes D (2012) *Creating Loving Attachments: Parenting with PACE to nurture confidence and security in the troubled child*, London: Jessica Kingsley Publishers

Habermas T and Bluck S (2000) 'Getting a life: The emergence of the life story in adolescence', *Psychological Bulletin*, 126:1, pp 748–769

Hammond S (2009) 'Updating life story work for use with a technologically proficient generation: a review', *Good Enough Caring Journal*, December, www.goodenoughcaring.com

Hammond S (2012) *Exploring a Role for Digital Technology in Life Story Work with Adolescents in Residential Care: A discourse analysis*, Doctoral thesis, University of East Anglia

Hammond S and Cooper N (2013) *Digital Life Story Work*, London: BAAF

Hammond S and Cooper N (2015) 'Embracing powerlessness in pursuit of digital resilience: managing cyber-literacy in professional talk', *Youth and Society*, 47:6, pp 769-788

Harper J (1996) 'Recapturing the past: alternative methods of life story work in adoption and fostering', *Adoption & Fostering*, 20:3, pp 21–28

Harris P (ed) (2006) *In Search of Belonging: Reflections by transracially adopted people*, London: BAAF

Harris P (ed) (2008) *The Colours in Me: Writing and Poetry by adopted children and young people*, London: BAAF

Harrison C, Lunzer E, Tymms P, Taylor Fitz-Gibbon C and Restorick J (2004) 'Use of ICT and its relationship with performance in examinations: a comparison of the ImpaCT2 project's research findings using pupil-level, school-level and multilevel modelling data', *Journal of Computer Assisted Learning*, 20:5, pp 319–337

Henry DL (2005) 'The 3-5-7 Model: preparing children for permanency', *Children and Youth Services Review*, 27:2, pp 197–212

Jewett Jarrett C (1979) *Adopting the Older Child*, Boston, MA: Harvard Common Press

Kulkofsky S and Koh JBK (2009) 'Why they reminisce: caregiver reports of the functions of joint reminiscence in early childhood', *Memory*, 17:4, pp 458–470

Livingston K and Condie R (2003) *Evaluation of the SCHOLAR Programme: Final report for the Scottish Executive Education Department*, Edinburgh: Scottish Executive

Mackrill T, Ebsen F and Antczak H (2015) 'Developing scales for smartphone applications together: youth and municipal case worker perspectives', *Advances in Social Work*, 16:1, pp. 67–77

McLean K (2005) 'Late adolescent identity development: narrative meaning making and memory telling', *Developmental Psychology*, 41:1, pp 683–691

Moffat F (2012) *Writing a Later Life Letter*, London: BAAF

Neil E, Beek M and Ward E (2015) *Contact after Adoption: A longitudinal study of post-adoption contact arrangements*, London: CoramBAAF

Nelson K and Fivush R (2004) 'The emergence of autobiographical memory: a social cultural developmental theory', *Psychological Review*, 111:1, pp 486–511

Northern Ireland Foster Care Association (1995) *Life Books for Children in Care*, Belfast: Northern Ireland Foster Care Association

NSPCC (2015) *12 Questions Answered about Parenting in the Digital Age*, available at: https://www.nspcc.org.uk/preventing-abuse/keeping-children-safe/online-safety/questions-parenting-digital-age/

Ofsted (2010) *The Safe Use of New Technologies*, available from: www.allertonbywater.leeds.sch.uk/upload/documents/e%20safety/the%20safe%20use%20of%20new%20technologies.pdf

Pallett C, Blackeby K, Yule W, Weissman R and Scott S (2011) *Fostering Changes: How to improve relationships and manage difficult behaviour*, London: BAAF

Rees J (2009) *Life Story Books for Adopted Children*, London: Jessica Kingsley Publishers

Sayers A and Roach R (2011) *Child Appreciation Days*, London: BAAF

Shah S and Argent H (2006) *Life Story Work: What it is and what it means*, London: BAAF

Schofield G and Beek M (2006) *Attachment Handbook for Foster Care and Adoption*, London: CoramBAAF

Shotton G (2012) *"Remember when": Exploring the experiences of looked after children and their carers in engaging in collaborative reminiscence*, Newcastle: University of Newcastle

Telenor Group (2013) *Building Digital Resilience*, available at: https://www.telenor.com/wp-content/uploads/2013/04/Telenor-report-Building-Digital-Resilience.pdf

Treacher A and Katz I (2001) 'Narrative and fantasy in adoption', *Adoption & Fostering*, 25:3, pp 20–28

Tregeagle S and Darcy M (2008) 'Child welfare and information and communication technology: today's challenge', *British Journal of Social Work*, 28, pp. 1481–1498

Further reading

To order any BAAF/CoramBAAF publication or for more information about these, visit www.corambaaf.org.uk/bookshop, where our whole range of publications is listed.

Adoption & Fostering, CoramBAAF's quarterly journal, frequently contains useful articles on life story work and related issues.

Adoption & Fostering 29:1 spring 2005, special edition on *listening to children*
This special bumper edition of *Adoption & Fostering*, guest edited by Caroline Thomas and Nigel Thomas, explores the theme of listening to children.

Archer C (1999) *First Steps in Parenting the Child who Hurts: Tiddlers and toddlers*, London: Jessica Kingsley Publishers

Archer C (1999) *Next Steps in Parenting the Child who Hurts: Tykes and teens*, London: Jessica Kingsley Publishers
Two helpful books, extremely practical and also drawing on current research into the physiological and psychological impact of childhood adversity.

Bowlby J (1982) *Loss, Sadness and Depression*, New York, NY: Basic Books
All Bowlby's work on attachment and loss needs to be revisited at regular intervals. He has been unjustly diminished and unjustly glorified; the work has weaknesses, but has proved immensely valuable.

Briere J (1992) *Child Abuse Trauma: Theory and treatment of the lasting effects*, Newbury Park, CA: Sage Publications
This important text should form part of any serious study of the subject.

Brodzinsky A, Smith D and Brodzinsky D (1998) *Children's Adjustment to Adoption: Developmental and clinical issues*, Thousand Oaks, CA: Sage Publications

Brodzinsky D (1984) 'Children's understanding of adoption', *Child Development*, 55, pp 869–878
Brodzinsky has undertaken extensive research into how children of different ages understand adoption.

Cairns K (2002) *Attachment, Trauma and Resilience: Therapeutic caring for children*, London: BAAF
Examines the realities of life with children who have lived through overwhelming stress, explores theories and research that may help make sense of this experience, and suggests ways in which carers and helpers can promote recovery and resilience.

Clark A and Statham J (2005) 'Listening to young children: experts in their own lives', *Adoption & Fostering*, 29:1, pp45–56
An interesting article explaining the mosaic approach.

Commission for Social Care Inspection (2006) *About Adoption: A children's views report*, London: Commission for Social Care Inspection

Durant S (2003) *Outdoor Play*, Leamington Spa: Step Forward Publishing

Fahlberg V (1994) *A Child's Journey Through Placement*, London: BAAF
An invaluable guide to many aspects of adoption.

Feast J and Philpot T (2003) *Searching Questions: Identity, origins and adoption*, London: BAAF
A book and video looking at the search and reunion experiences of adopted adults, adoptive parents and birth parents.

Gilligan R (2007) *Promoting Resilience: A resource guide on working with children in the care system* (2nd edition), London: BAAF
Full of practical ideas for improving the quality of life for looked after children, addressing key relationships and settings through which resilience may be enhanced.

Grotevant H and McRoy R (1998) *Openness in Adoption: Exploring family connections*, Thousand Oaks, CA: Sage Publications

Hellett J and Smith G (2003) *Parenting a Child who has been Sexually Abused*, London: BAAF
A book and video, designed for training and discussion in small groups of adopters or foster carers.

Howe D and Feast J (2003) *Adoption, Search and Reunion*, London: BAAF
A study looking at the search and reunion process.

Jewett Jarratt C (1997) *Helping Children Cope with Separation and Loss*, London: BAAF/Batsford
A useful discussion of the effect of grief on behaviour, with exercises to do with children and advice to carers.

Karr-Morse R and Wiley M S (1997) *Ghosts from the Nursery: The origins of violent behaviour*, New York, NY: Atlantic Monthly Press
Readable, accessible and relatively inexpensive, this highly recommended book explores the origins of much that is puzzling in the behaviour of children who have suffered early adversity.

Kirk H D (1964) *Shared Fate*, New York: Free Press

Lacher D, Nichols T and May J (2005) *Connecting with Kids through Stories*, London: Jessica Kingsley Publishers
A book on the use of stories therapeutically to help children attach to adopters.

Lindon J (2006) *Helping Babies and Toddlers Learn: A guide to good practice with under-threes* (second ed), London: National Children's Bureau

Morris J (2002) *A lot to say!*
Available free to download from www.scope.org.uk
A helpful free guide for social workers, personal advisors and others

working with disabled children and young people with communication impairments.

Morrison M (2012) *Talking about Adoption to your Adopted Child*, London: BAAF
A practical handbook for adopters.

Neil E, Beek M and Ward E (2015) *Contact after Adoption: A longitudinal study of post-adoption contact arrangments*, London: CoramBAAF

Oaklander V (1978) *Windows to our Children: a Gestalt therapy approach to children and adults*, Boulder, CO: Real People Press
A practical therapeutic guide to working with children and young people, giving insight into how they interpret the traumas they experience. Valuable for all professionals working with children.

O'Malley B (2000) *Lifebooks: Creating a treasure for the adopted child*, Winthrop, MA: Adoption Works
Order on www.adoptionlifebooks.com
An overview which also gives practical examples of what to include. Helpful, although a little "Americanised" and slightly more geared to intercountry adoption.

Plummer D (2005) *Helping Adolescents and Adults to Build Self-Esteem*, London: Jessica Kingsley Publishers
A photocopiable resource book with some relevant pages for life story work.

Prevatt-Goldstein B and Spencer M (2000) *Race and Ethnicity: A consideration of issues for black, minority ethnic and white children in family placement*, London: BAAF
A practice guide examining practice experience, the legal framework in the UK, and research findings about family placement.

Romaine M, Turley T and Tuckey N (2007) *Preparing Children for Permanence*, London: BAAF
A practical guide for social workers, carers and parents on undertaking direct work with children being prepared for a move to a new permanent family.

Rose R and Philpot T (2005) *The Child's Own Story*, London: Jessica Kingsley Publishers
A good outline of life story work with useful tips and help on planning and the process.

Schofield G (2005) 'The voice of the child in family placement decision-making', *Adoption & Fostering*, 29:1, pp29–44
An excellent article explaining how to make sense of the child's views on, for example, contact and placements.

Schofield G and Beek M (2006) *Attachment Handbook for Foster Care and Adoption*, London: BAAF
A comprehensive handbook that provides an explanation of core

attachment concepts, using vivid case examples to make connections with the daily life of adoptive and foster families.

Sgroi S (1982, new edition 1993) 'Treatment of the sexually abused children' in Sgroi S (ed), *Handbook of Clinical Intervention in Child Sexual Abuse*, Lexington, MA: Lexington Books
Looks at issues in child sexual abuse such as investigation, credibility assessment, victim and family treatment, and therapy. The 1993 edition contains new chapters on medical evaluation, working with male victims and play group therapy.

Smith G (1991) 'The unbearable traumatic past' in Varma V (ed), *The Secret Lives of Vulnerable Children*, London: Routledge

Smith G (2008) *The Protector's Handbook*, London: BAAF
A handbook which should be compulsory reading before plans are made for children.

Smith G (2005) 'Children's narratives of traumatic experiences', in Vetere A and Dowling E (eds) *Narrative Therapies with Children and their Families: A practitioner's guide to concepts and approaches*, London: Routledge

Sunderland M, Armstrong N and Hancock N, *Helping Children with Feelings* series, Brackley: Speechmark Publications
Various books, including:
   Sunderland M and Hancock N (1999) *Helping Children with Low Self-Esteem*
   Sunderland M and Hancock N (1999) *Helping Children who Bottle up their Feelings*
   Sunderland M and Hancock N (2003) *Helping Children Locked in Rage or Hate*
   Sunderland M and Hancock N (2003) *Helping Children with Loss*

Troyna B and Hatcher R (1992) *Racism in Children's Lives: A study of mainly white primary schools*, London: Routledge/National Children's Bureau
This book, based on extensive interviews with black and white children in their last two years of primary schooling, is a fascinating study of how "race" emerges for young children as a plausible explanatory framework for incidents in their everyday lives.

Van der Kolk B, McFarlane A and Weisaeth L (eds) (1996) *Traumatic Stress: The effects of overwhelming experience on mind, body and society*, New York, NY: Guilford Press
A definitive collection of papers on the understanding of the effects of traumatic stress on children and adults.

Wilson A N (1980) *The Development of Psychology of the Black Child*, New York: African Research Publication

Wolin SJ and Wolin S (1993) *The Resilient Self: How survivors of troubled families rise above adversity*, New York, NY: Villard Books
A fascinating outline of work on children who manage to do 'a very lot with a very little'.